Down Ratra Road

Fifty Years of Civil Defence in Ireland

PADRAIC O'FARRELL

Published by
THE STATIONERY OFFICE

To be purchased directly from the
GOVERNMENT PUBLICATIONS SALES OFFICE,
SUN ALLIANCE HOUSE,
MOLESWORTH STREET, DUBLIN 2

or by mail order from
GOVERNMENT PUBLICATIONS,
POSTAL TRADE SECTION,
4-5 HARCOURT STREET, DUBLIN 2.
TEL: 01 647 6834/35/36/37, FAX: 01 475 2760
or through any bookseller.

Set in 11pt on 12.5pt Adobe Caslon

ISBN 0-7076-6506-X

ORIGINATION AND DESIGN
Susan Waine

PRINTED IN IRELAND
by ßetaprint Limited, Dublin

Contents

ACKNOWLEDGEMENTS

I wish to thank the following members of the staff of the Civil Defence School: Oliver O' Sullivan for his research and for unfailing and prompt assistance in obtaining requested information, Eamonn Farrell, for his advice and for checking the draft of this work and Fergus Mulcahy for his observations on the manuscript. Valerie Ingram, Librarian, and Edel Kirby and Bill in the Registry of the Office of Public Works gave tremendous assistance as did the staffs of National Archives Ireland, The National Library of Ireland, The Gilbert Library, Westmeath County Library and Telford College Library, Edinburgh.

I thank Professor John Montague for his permission to quote from *The Rough Field* (Mountrath 1972) and Raven Press and Conleth Ellis for the excerpt from *After Doomsday*. The excerpt from *My Early Life* is reproduced with permission of Curtis Brown Ltd, London, on behalf of the Estate of Sir Winston S. Churchill; copyright Winston S. Churchill. Gill & Macmillan, Dublin kindly gave permission for the extract from Elizabeth Shannon's *Up in the Park* (1983) and for use of the Philip Conran photograph from Bernard Share's *The Emergency* (1978) on page 7. Thanks also to *An Cosantóir* and the Air Corps Photographic Section (Papal visit), the *Irish Examiner* (Northern refugees) and *Galway Now* (one jacket figure) for their permission to use photographs.

Thanks to of The National Gallery of Ireland for use of their photograph of Mr Douglas Hyde and to The National Library of Ireland for that of Sir Winston S. Churchill.

Cartoons are reproductions of those contributed to issues of *Irisleabhar na Cosanta Sibhialta* by Michael Byrne, a former Executive Officer in the Civil Defence School.

Sister Philomena of Loreto College, Mullingar and Lt Col Con Costello set me on the road for information on Firmount House. Sister Juliana Dussel, archivist at North America IBVM, Loretto Abbey, Toronto supplied information on Teresa Dease that Sister Kathleen McGovern and the late Lena Boylan, Trustee of Castletown House, Headquarters of the Irish Georgian Society, Celbridge, County Kildare had researched.

The Army Press Office, the Military Archives, Comdt Steve Noonan, Comdt S. Cloonan and other staff members of the Radiological Monitoring Section at Defence Forces Headquarters and Comdt Padraic McDunphy were also willing and prompt in providing information.

Others who helped were Joe Campbell who contributed recollections of the late Sylvester FitzPatrick, John Curran, Micheál Ó Gabhláin , Lt Col Maurice Shanahan, Fergal Tobin, Peggy Joyce, Lilian Enright, Tom Casserley, Margaret Hogg, Noel O' Beara, Patsy Sheridan, Ian McDonald, Brian Gillen and Seamus O'Brien.

As usual, my wife Maureen assisted with proof-reading while my daughter Niamh took on some word-processing.

PADRAIC O'FARRELL, 2000

The views expressed in this book are those of the author and do not represent official Department of Defence policy.

Message from the Minister for Defence

I am delighted to be associated with the publication of this book written by Padraic O'Farrell. Padraic has traced the history of Civil Defence in Ireland from its establishment in December 1950 to the present day. Having served as a Regional Civil Defence Officer himself from 1977 to 1980 he was in an unique position to draw together many of the interesting events that have marked the development of the organization over the past fifty years.

My early memories of Civil Defence were of volunteers trained to deal with the consequences of a nuclear war. With the diminution of the Cold War threat, the organization changed its focus to concentrate on assisting Local Authorities in developing local community services. It can be said with pride that Civil Defence is fast developing the capacity to provide a first class second line emergency service for local communities.

I want to thank all those who have helped make Civil Defence what it is today and, in particular, the thousands of volunteers who have given, and continue to give, freely of their own time for the betterment of others. This is the hallmark of the organization and long may it continue.

I was especially pleased to achieve Government approval for a significant increase in funding for Civil Defence purposes in the year 2000 and I am committed to continuing this level of support in the future to ensure that Civil Defence has the funding to acquire the best equipment that this organization deserves.

Ar son an Rialtais, ar mo shon féin agus ar son an Aire Stáit, Séamus Ó Braonán, ba mhaith liom buíochas a gabháil le gach uile dhuine a raibh baint acu le Cosaint Shibhialta le caoga bliain anuas.

MICHAEL SMITH, T.D.
Minister for Defence

Message from the Minister of State at the Department of Defence

As Minister of State at the Department of Defence, with special responsibility for Civil Defence, I am pleased to be associated with the publication of Padraic O'Farrell's book on the history and times of Civil Defence.

On reading this book I am reminded of the commitment and dedication of Civil Defence volunteers past and present. Volunteers are the backbone of the organization and deserve the highest praise for giving freely of their time, particularly now that the Irish economy is booming and opportunities in paid employment are available nationwide.

The management of Civil Defence, including County Controllers and Civil Defence Officers, deserve much praise for steering the organization through the last fifty years by ensuring that it has the personnel, the training and the equipment to meet new challenges. The staff of the Department of Defence who, down the years, have been very supportive of Civil Defence also deserve a special word of thanks. I know that strong friendships have developed and mutual respect has been the winner.

To underpin the changing nature of the challenges facing the organization, I am pleased to say the Government recently approved the Heads of a new Civil Defence Bill which will be published in the near future. This Bill will update and improve existing legislation in relation to Civil Defence and steer the organization through the early stages of this new millennium.

Throughout the years the organization has truly lived up to its motto 'when it counts, we're there' and I am confident that the many Civil Defence members, who proudly wear the distinctive yellow uniforms, will be even more prominent at local and national events in the years ahead.

Caoga bliain ag fás, caoga bliain thar barr, caoga míle buíochas.

SÉAMUS BRENNAN, T.D.
Minister of State

Celebrating Service

'Our remedies oft in ourselves do lie,
Which we ascribe to heaven'
(SHAKESPEARE: *All's Well that Ends Well*
Act I Scene I)

I

Genesis

LONDON'S BLITZ AND THE NORTH STRAND BOMBING

From 1939 to 1945, Europe was in turmoil, enduring a war that was causing destruction on a scale never experienced previously. Civilian populations, especially in cities, suffered enormously. There were thousands of situations requiring trained experts in rescue, welfare, warden and casualty treatment. The London Blitz, that lasted from September 1940 until May 1941 provided many. The author, J.B. Priestly said of this period of intense bombing: 'Britain... is now being bombed and burned into democracy.'

And why?

'The Home Guard, the Observer Corps, all the ARP [Air Raid Precautions personnel] and fire-fighting services, and the like... what might be called the organized militant citizen... the circumstances of their war-time life favour a sharply democratic outlook.'

Men and women who had worn stiff upper lips and dined at their clubs while their sons squandered part of their fortunes at Oxford and Cambridge; who had tea and crumpet on the vicar's croquet green – these people suddenly became stretcher-bearers and tea makers and ladder carriers and even fine leaders in the various services.

Wartime plans for civil defence envisaged sudden daylight bombings that would be intense but of short duration. Public and private shelters were not designed for long occupancy, nor even for overnight periods. At the height of the Blitz those same plans assumed that occupants of the blast ravaged East End slums should be dead. They were not, and when this became clear the Heavy Rescue Service went on twenty-four hour shifts removing survivors. They found one girl who had remained buried in rubble for 107 hours. When rescued, she was alive and well but she held a dead baby in her arms. Commentators reckoned that ten per cent of all bombs dropped were unexploded and an UXB was a dangerous and frightening hazard.

Each day saw throngs of people leaving the city for outlying towns. At their destination, close on a thousand might be accommodated in a large factory or cinema in the suburbs or further afield. Wardens gallantly tried to quell fear and anger. Rescue and Casualty volunteers brought survivors to rest centres, where Welfare workers organized accommodation and care.

Winston Churchill tried to whip up morale. 'Statisticians may amuse themselves by calculating that after making allowance for the working of the law of diminishing returns, through the same house being struck twice or three times over, it would take ten years at the present rate, for half the houses of London to be demolished. After that, of course, progress would be much slower.'

Both conventional and incendiary bombs fell and parachutes delivered mines.

'DON'T LIGHT THAT FAG!'

Nerves were becoming frayed. 'Don't light that fag out there! The Jerries [Germans] might see it.'

'Let's go into that bombed out shop for a little bit – don't you know they never bomb the same building twice.'

Distribution of one and a half million family shelters began, courtesy of Sir John Anderson, Home Secretary and Minister for Home Security. Residents who owned gardens received them. An 'Anderson Shelter' comprised two curved walls of corrugated steel bolted to metal rails, sunk three feet into the ground and covered with earth. It could protect six people from all but a direct hit and it cost seven pounds if you did not pass the 'means test' for a free issue.

Communal brick shelters followed – many of them without mortar, due to an error in the Government form of contract. But the underground rail stations provided the most popular shelter and strains of 'We'll meet Again', 'White Cliffs of Dover' and 'Run Rabbit Run' filled platforms on the Bakerloo-Cockfoster line. Beleaguered folk abandoned prejudices and privacy and double-barreled names were as useless as double-barreled shotguns against the battering assault from the clouds.

Wardens became adept at acting as masters of ceremonies for impromptu entertainments. These took place between news bulletins and Lord Haw Haw's German propaganda broadcasts. Officialdom warned against 'deep shelter mentality' setting in if citizens persisted in using the underground.

The ARP services tried to cope. When the Blitz ended, a Southwark ARP leader was asked to nominate some of his Heavy Rescue squad for medals. He replied, 'Medals? We don't want no medals. The whole borough deserves a medal.' And that was telling them!

WAITING IN DREAD

In neutral Ireland, people listened to the wireless and followed the course of the war as long as their 'wet' and 'dry' batteries allowed reception. They worried and prayed for relatives and for the general public in London and in other UK cities.

The Governing Body of *Saorstát Éireann*, The Irish Free State, from December 6th 1922 to December 29th 1937 was known as the Executive Council. It allotted responsibility for air raid precautions to the Defence Forces. That was in 1936 and two army officers went to England to study the situation. They submitted a report in 1937. Subsequently, Ireland's ARP Act of 1939 made Local Authorities responsible for taking precautions with the object of protecting persons and property in the event of an attack from the air. Maynooth and Clongowes Wood Colleges were earmarked as base hospitals for possible casualties from a Dublin raid. Auxiliary hospitals at Ballinasloe and Mallow were also selected.

Before that, some public bodies had submitted ARP schemes to the Department of Defence. Army searchlights probed murky skies and schoolboys in a remote rural school obeyed 'The Master' and packed cement filler into the hewn name plaque that proclaimed it was *Scoil Naomh Mhuire, Baile an t-Séipéil*. Some invading German soldier might know Irish, you see!

Dublin, on the East Coast, was particularly vulnerable and its Corporation installed air raid sirens in thirty-nine locations, so that everybody in the city would hear one of them. It set up an ARP Central Control in Lord Edward Street. Its Emergency Communications Service would come into operation if a breakdown in normal services occurred. An Auxiliary Fire Service (AFS) would support each regular brigade. Other services began to appear – Casualty, Rescue, Decontamination, Demolition and Repair. Some of them would become familiar to Civil Defence volunteers a dozen years later.

'We are a small nation with a chequered history and in a world of warring nations our community should be a haven of peace, a community of goodwill.' So spoke Sean Moylan, the Parliamentary Secretary to the Minister for Defence after the outbreak of war. He was broadcasting about taking precautions against air raids. The Air Raid Precautions Act of 1939 provided for a network of centres to train the civilian population in methods of coping with air attacks.

On September 4th 1939, Dublin Corporation announced plans to train Air Raid Wardens. Sessions would take place at the Town Hall, Rathmines, the Mansion House, Bolton Street Technical School, the Central Model School and the National School on Howth Road. A group of dedicated volunteers

North Strand, general scene around the bomb crater

Searching for casualties in a demolished building

imparted instruction. They had prepared for their task at the Air Raid Precautions School in Griffith Barracks, Dublin. That institution developed from an earlier Civilian Anti-Gas School.

This 'flash-light' picture gives some idea of the early work of the services, where in darkened streets they had to fight fires, search for and rescue casualties

Up to 170 aircraft crashed or force landed in Ireland during the war, killing 223 airmen. Despite this, many regarded precautions against air raids with cynicism, apathy or plain jocularity. A Dublin newspaper boasted about its civic spirit in observing the 'black out' by using window blinds, while a county Kildare farmer cut the two ends from a large cocoa tin to form a cylinder for putting over his burning Sacred Heart lamp!

A Focke-Wulf WF 200C-1 bomber crashed at Faha Mountain, County Kerry, on August 20th 1940. Six days later the first bombs fell on neutral Ireland. At Campile and Ambrosetown, County Wexford, two aircraft dropped four bombs on each location. Three female employees of the Shelbourne Cooperative were killed.

Bombs fell on Dublin's south city on two successive nights of January 1941, but caused little damage. Then came one of our more noble moments in North-South cooperation. When the big 'Easter Tuesday Air Raid' of Belfast occurred on April 15th 1941, Dun Laoghaire, Dublin, Drogheda and Dundalk fire brigades rushed north to fight the fires. Bill Morrison's fine play, *The Emperor of Ice Cream*, from the novel by Brian Moore vividly recalls the event in which 700 were killed and 1,511 injured.

Damage from the third
bomb

The New York correspondent of the *Daily Telegraph* said, 'A wave of gratitude for Éire's errand of mercy has swept [Belfast] overnight, establishing a bond of sympathy between North and South of Ireland which no British or Irish Statesman has been able to establish in a generation.'

THE NORTH STRAND

It was but a short distance from the ARP's Howth Road training centre to the location of Dublin's biggest wartime bombing incident. It occurred in May 1941. ARP Warden and Rescue Services were prominent at that disaster. They were the forerunners of Civil Defence.

Although bombs fell in other areas of Dublin on the same night, the event went down in folklore as 'The North Strand Bombing'. It was the only suspicious bombardment. Some commentators suggested that it represented a German warning to the country not to supply the UK with farm produce.

Between midnight and 4 a.m. on May 31st 1941, four bombs fell. One, of 250 pounds, hit the North Circular Road-North Richmond Street area at 01.30 hours. It did little damage to living accommodation, destroying only the house on which it landed and causing fire damage in an adjacent one. Gas and water mains, water and electricity transformers suffered extensively, however. There were no fatal casualties, but a man buried in rubble received severe injuries.

A hundred yards away, at Summerhill Parade, another bomb fell, demolishing two houses. One seriously injured woman died later. A rescue team pulled two other women from the debris.

Near the Phoenix Park pumping station, at 02.00 hours, a bomb fell. It destroyed one house and trapped its occupants. They later escaped, with minor injuries. The same bomb caused further damage to water and gas mains.

The biggest bomb, of 500 pounds, fell on the North Strand. It destroyed twenty-five houses and damaged forty-five so badly that they had to be demolished later. Up to 300 homes became unfit for habitation and 1,000 needed repairs of a minor nature. The bomb killed twenty-eight people and wounded forty-five.

Some critics have decried the performance of the ARP during Dublin's night of horror but fair-minded, responsible people who were on the scene have repeatedly vouched for their highly commendable work.

In September 1941, the Neutrality (War Damage to Property) Act became law and Dublin Corporation set up War Damage Depots for salvaging household effects, removing and storing furniture from damaged buildings and rendering 'structural first aid' to homes in the event of further bombings. Routes of evacuation

from Dublin and Cork to rural areas in the event of further bomb-ings were determined also.

The Lord Mayor, Martin O'Sullivan issued a handbook in 1944. It showed that by then each Municipal Council had provid-ed a large number of protective trenches, had reinforced base-ments and built over-ground public shelters. These had sanitary facilities, artificial light and drinking water. Graffiti had not arrived in cities then, but the long, ugly installations were a boon to posters advertising dances, gymkhanas, fetes and even 'liquid stockings'.

Some spectators use O'Connell Street air-raid shelters to view a military parade (1942)

GERMAN DOCUMENTS

When the Allies reached Brussels in 1945, they unearthed certain documents in the Institut Cartographique Militaire, the German

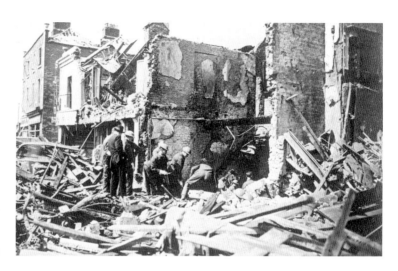

Searching for casualties

Staff's map-making centre. Some of these were categorized
'Militar Geographische Angaben uber Irland'. They contained a
vast amount of detail and diagrams. Sections included headings
translated as General Outline, Description of Particular Districts,
Particular Data, Historical Background and Communications.
They contained inaccuracies and rash observations too, with the
Boyne rising in the Slieve Blooms and the southern half of Kerry
belonging, politically, to Cork! A Stadplan von Dublin gave little
precise information and could have been about almost any other
city in Europe.

The war's ultimate horrific termination when atomic bombs
were dropped on Hiroshima and Nagasaki underlined the necessity for a Civil Defence Service but first-hand experience at home
had already signalled the requirement.

Many years later, the Department of Defence and the Civil
Defence School realized the significance of the North Strand
story as a stimulus for action. They published a booklet on the
subject that accompanied an illustrated talk. Its conclusion provides an apt note upon which to end:

YOUR DUTY

This story of what happened in Dublin on May 31st 1941 demon-
strates the necessity for an *organized and trained body of civilians* –
giving voluntary service – to cope with any possible disaster of this
nature in the future.

Civil Defence will provide the means to this end.

2

Brief History of Civil Defence

'BABIES SATISFACTORILY BORN'

On July 16th 1945, the President of the United States of America (USA), Harry S. Truman, received information on the successful testing of an atomic bomb at Alamogordo, New Mexico. The coded message said 'Babies satisfactorily born'. At 8.15 a.m. on August 6th 1945, a United States Air Force B-29 plane, the *Enola Gay* dropped an atomic bomb on Hiroshima. Three days later another fell on Nagasaki. Reported casualties numbered 140,000 dead and 70,000 injured. The former cities were piles of rubble. World War Two formally ended on September 2nd when General MacArthur, as Supreme Commander of the Allied Forces, signed the Japanese surrender document delivered to him on board the *U.S.S. Missouri*. The world relaxed, but began asking questions.

In Ireland, the Defence Forces began discharging those who had answered the call during 'The Emergency'. Local Authorities were abandoning emergency planning and demobilizing the voluntary ARP organization. Some of its personnel had been part of the Local Security Force (LSF), that later, in 1947, became absorbed in a new Second Line Reserve, An Fórsa Cosanta Áitiúil (FCA).

The hopes expressed in Vera Lynn's song 'When the Lights go on again All Over the World' had been realized. Irish schoolboys were on ladders again, chipping away the cement filler and restoring the names of their educational establishments. The celebration of peace had barely subsided when a new threat began causing grave concern. As part of their post-war agreements, the victorious Allies had divided the city of Berlin. British, French and American zones collectively would become known later as West Berlin. The sector occupied by Union of Soviet Socialist Republics (USSR/Soviet Union/Russia) would form East Berlin. The division eventually became a major issue in a political and economic struggle between the capitalist, democratic West and the Soviet-led East. The conflict became known as the Cold War and nations began fearing it could lead to a situation signalling Doomsday.

The USSR imposed a land and water blockade of West Berlin. For months, Western powers carried out major airlifts of supplies to beleaguered inhabitants. A more sinister issue was the successful testing of an atomic bomb by the USSR in 1948. Now the world had two hostile superpowers, each developing its nuclear technology. The UK had an active Civil Defence Service during the war. Fully disbanded in 1945, the shiver of Cold War led to its hasty reconstitution.

In China, during 1945-6, Mao Tse-tung had resumed the Communist struggle against the Nationalists of Chiang Kai-shek, switching from guerrilla warfare to set battles. His forces entered Peking in October 1949 and he accepted office as Chairman of the People's Republic of China. The chasm between West and East was growing.

THE EARLY 1950S

Ireland's general population did not care much. They took holidays in Tramore or Salthill and ambitious couples spent honeymoons in Bournemouth or Llandudno. If they ventured towards the French Riviera, they were really posh. In Dublin, an afternoon gliding the maple floor of the Metropole to Phil Murtagh's music and an evening dancing to Carmel Quinn's crooning in the Crystal Ballroom could lead to a late night tennis-club hop and perhaps a date. That constituted a wild night out.

On February 26th 1952, the British Prime Minister, Winston Churchill, informed the House of Commons that Britain had a plant capable of producing an atomic bomb and that a test would take place within the year. It did, on October 3rd in the Monte Bello islands, off the northwest coast of Australia. In November of the same year, the USA exploded the first Hydrogen bomb on Eniwetok, an atoll in the Pacific Islands. An eyewitness claimed that a nearby island disappeared in the blast. The H-bomb's power came from the release of energy locked in the nucleus of the atom. Thermo nuclear weapons had arrived. Ireland was watching another kind of violence. John Wayne as Sean Thornton was fighting for Maureen O'Hara, playing Mary Kate Danaher in John Ford's film *The Quiet Man*.

The Korean War of 1950-3 was then in progress. It had its origins in rival claims for sovereignty over a unified peninsula. Asserting them, were the USSR sponsored People's Democratic Republic in the North and the Republic of Korea, supported by the United States of America, in the South.

So a maelstrom of situations involving superpowers armed with super bombs was filling nations with trepidation.

TAKING NOTE

During all this time, the Irish Government was taking note. Caring for a community after any major disaster would demand teams skilled in first aid, fire fighting, rescue, evacuation and catering procedures. An added nuclear factor would demand new skills. A competent Civil Defence organization, trained for dealing with a nuclear situation in particular, was a basic requirement.

As early as December 20th 1950, at the request of the Minister for Defence, T.F. O'Higgins T.D., City and County Managers attended a meeting at Department of Defence headquarters in Dublin. The Minister issued a statement instructing Managers to prepare plans for a wartime situation. He pointed out that the provisions in the Air Raid Precautions Acts of 1939 and 1946 were not just temporary emergency measures; they formed part of the national permanent defence structure. They empowered the establishment of Civil Defence services.

REQUIREMENTS

The Minister's statement required each Local Authority to appoint a Civil Defence Officer (CDO). He would undertake the task of reconstituting and adapting the defunct ARP organization. Emphasis would be on rescue and casualty treatment and, as history would verify, a welfare service would be of the utmost importance. Each County Medical Officer of Health, County Engineer and Chief Fire Officer would take on casualty, rescue

Students and Staff at the first Civil Defence Officers Course, June 18th to 22nd 1951

An early 'Manpack' light rescue team ready for action.

and AFS leadership roles within Civil Defence. Two other senior staff members would act as Chief County Warden and Community Welfare Officer.

THE SCHOOL

Meanwhile, selected personnel were occupying Ratra House in the Phoenix Park. These included newly appointed Technical Officers for future staffing of a Civil Defence School. Some had to rush their turkey dinner at Christmas and forfeit celebrating the eve of the half-century. They began a course at The Civil Defence College, Easingwold, Yorkshire on January 1st 1951. Things were moving at a fast pace.

By summer, the Civil Defence School was ready to welcome its first students. Twenty-six newly appointed CDOs attended the first course, opened on June 18th 1951 by Oscar Traynor T.D., Minister for Defence in a five-day-old Government. The course would train CDOs to:

1. Establish Civil Defence in specified towns.
2. Select premises that were adequately protected and suitable for occupation by the Local Authority in the event of the outbreak of war.
3. Be responsible for their furnishing and equipment at short notice.
4. Organize stockpiling of ample quantities of articles required by each of the five services, all to be available at short notice. The Civil Defence School would purchase some items and distribute them; the CDO would acquire the remainder locally.

As soon as the course ended, they returned home and began recruiting. Two volunteers per thousand people in large centres of population and units of about thirty elsewhere were the targets. Candidates for Instructor courses at the Civil Defence School emerged and by the end of March 1952, over 100 had qualified. These began imparting instruction locally, establishing core groups capable of expanding rapidly in an emergency.

The Department of Defence began purchasing fire pumps, rescue vehicles, protective clothing, footwear and equipment for catering, rest centres and local training. Such expenditure in a stagnant economy when emigration had reached its highest level in half a century bore testimony to serious security fears.

Sean O'Donnell and his daughter Mary in Galway Rescue Unit in 1958

THE NUCLEAR AGE

Cold War strategists of the Western world were experimenting further. There were developments in the hydrogen or thermonuclear bomb. Superpowers were testing explosions in Megatons (millions of tons) rather than Kilotons (thousands) of trinitrotoluene (TNT). On March 1st 1954, the USA tested a second H-bomb at Bikini atoll, also in the Pacific Islands. At more than ten Megatons, it was 600 times more powerful than what fell on Hiroshima. Inhabitants of the Marshall Islands, hundreds of miles downwind of the test site, experienced radiation illnesses.

A Japanese trawler, ironically called *Lucky Dragon*, had been fishing seventy miles from Bikini and outside the prohibited zone. The craft and crew became heavily contaminated from what they described as 'white ash from the sun rising in the west'. This was radioactive dust dropping from a cloud that had mushroomed upwards from the blast area before drifting in the wind. The dreaded words 'nuclear fallout' had arrived in the vocabulary of defence policy and the world became aware of its being just as lethal as the blast, heat and immediate radiation from the bomb.

Furthermore, it was no longer necessary to consider carrying these bombs in planes. Long-range missiles could deliver destruction with accuracy from prepared sites to targets almost anywhere in the world. These would be part of any future conflict and their warheads would be capable of delivering high explosives, chemical gases, biological viruses or radioactivity.

There could be deliberate or accidental direct hits on Irish cities, or radioactive dust could spread from UK or European targets to any part of the country.

RADIOACTIVE DUST

There were few motor cars on the streets of country towns then and a man with a flat cap could find a dozen parking places in Dublin by directing you to 'Lock Hard!' Young people were beginning to enjoy the music of show-bands and other novel attractions. Yet, Civil Defence was able to convince many of them that the nuclear situation was serious and threatened both urban and rural populations. Even those already adept in fire fighting, first aid, evacuation, allotting accommodation and feeding following conventional bombing needed further instruction. To avoid exposure to fatal doses of radiation volunteers needed new rescue techniques. Man-packs would be required where vehicles bearing equipment had no freedom of movement. Advising the public on how to avoid the effects of fallout was a requirement. Furthermore, conventional wartime procedures envisaged transportation of rural volunteer teams to assist stricken urban residents. A nuclear fallout situation might make this impossible.

One incident brought the danger home unequivocally. Some countries were experimenting with or developing nuclear power stations for energy supplies. In 1957, the first nuclear accident with off-site risks occurred in one of these; close to Ireland too, at Windscale, later Sellafield, in Cumbria. The plant was a mere 130 kilometres from Strangford and 200 from the heart of Dublin.

WINDSCALE

Atomic piles had begun operating at Windscale in October 1950 and in less than two years the plant had produced the first plutonium manufactured in the UK. Earlier that year, scientists had deliberately discharged large amounts of radioactivity from the plant into the Irish Sea. There were allegations that, in 1956, they raised these to observe the results. During the following year an accidental fire caused release of radioactivity and severe core damage at the station. Partial implementation of local emergency plans at Windscale followed. At one stage, three tonnes of uranium were blazing. It took three days to bring the fire under control.

In 1957, Civil Defence volunteers received a handbook called *Methods of Protection*. It advised on means of sheltering families and livestock from the dangerous dust. It told how the Government, through Civil Defence and the Defence Forces, would inform, advise and warn the population. In the case of a direct strike, mobile columns would move people out of the lethal radiation area, known as the Z- zone, into less dangerous localities.

It became obvious that the Civil Defence Warden Service (see Warden Service) needed massive expansion – hundreds in each county.

MINISTER'S SPEECH

Early in 1957, a radio appeal from the Minister for Defence encouraged more citizens to join Civil Defence. Advertisements appeared in national newspapers. A May meeting in the Mansion

An early rescue vehicle originally used in the Lonbon blitz. Noel O'Beara holds its starting handle

House, Dublin aimed at recruiting new members. One hundred and fifty out of the 500 attending enlisted. The penny had dropped with an alarming clang. People, including former sceptics, were at last taking the nuclear threat seriously.

PROGRESS

The first course for Warden Instructors at the Civil Defence School was in September 1957. The following year, the School published Warden Training Notes in booklet form and issued copies to all Local Authorities. Progress reported in February 1st 1958 was encouraging. Volume 1, Number 3 of the *Civil Defence Bulletin* stated:

> Just a year ago the call went out for volunteers to man the Civil Defence services. This was the first intimation the general public received that such an organization was being contemplated, although many recognised the dangers inherent in the development of nuclear weapons.... During the past year 3,000 volunteers have come forward. Training has commenced and is proceeding in most areas

In 1958 too, the construction of training ranges in locations around the country was nearing completion. The Gas Van, a mobile gas chamber for training personnel in respirator use and testing, continued to tour the country.

Meanwhile, on October 4th 1957, the USSR had become the first to launch a man-made satellite. Every ninety-five minutes the 'artificial moon', Sputnik 1, was orbiting 500 miles above the

Eamon deValera, (Uachtarán na hÉireann), taking the salute from Civil Defence Volunteers during the Easter Parade, 1960

earth. Its speed was 18,000 miles per hour. The USSR's Lunik programme was collecting data on radiation and other matter in space. Its Lunik 2 spacecraft crash-landed on the moon on September 14th 1959.

THE WALL AND THE WONDERING

Ending a 156 year tradition, the last Grand Canal barge loaded with casks of Guinness set off from James's Street Harbour for Limerick in May 1960. At the end of the year, the Boeing aircraft, *St Patrick*, completed *Aer Lingus's* first jet flight. Ireland's 'Come day, go day; God send Sunday' slow progress attitude was ending. The 'Swinging Sixties' had taken a hold with all its laughter, love and long hair.

On April 17th 1961 there was an unsuccessful invasion of Cuba by USA backed Cuban exiles. It aimed at ousting Fidel Castro's Communist regime. The debacle became known as the Bay of Pigs Invasion, because its shore provided a landing area on the island. Four months later, East Berlin erected the Berlin Wall. It became a physical reminder of the confrontational situation existing between East and West. Communism was spreading in Africa, South America and East Asia. The USA had plans for putting a man on the moon. Resulting space programme technology was further improving the potential range, accuracy and destructive power of nuclear missiles.

In Ireland, the Department of Defence nominated County Managers as County Controllers of Civil Defence. Courses for Scientific Intelligence Officers (SIOs) began at the Civil Defence School in February 1962. These were designed to train key personnel in advising County Controllers on scientific aspects of Civil Defence, such as processing radiological information.

Both Civil Defence and the Army Observer Corps were viewing locations that would, in a nuclear situation, serve as a Temporary Integrated National Control. Montrose House in Donnybrook, Dublin was in contention for a while, but the basement of the Department of Defence Headquarters on Infirmary Road became first choice.

CUBA

During the spring and summer of 1962 the USSR was involving itself in Cuban affairs. It was obvious that more than learning how to rumba was taking place, so Washington began questioning. On September 2nd, the Soviet Government admitted that it was supplying arms to Cuba, but a week later denied that they were for offensive purposes. Aerial reconnaissance by American aircraft convinced President Kennedy that forty-two ballistic missiles, with atomic warheads, were being installed. These were capable of reaching any city in the United States.

On October 22nd, Kennedy announced his intention of imposing a naval blockade on Cuba and formally requested the removal of all missiles from the island. Four days later, the Soviet Prime Minister, Nikita Khrushchev, offered to withdraw the missiles if North Atlantic Treaty Organisation (NATO) forces acted similarly in Turkey. Kennedy rejected the suggestion. A grave risk of war existed until October 28th. Khrushchev agreed to remove the weapons under United Nations Organization (UNO) supervision, provided the USA lifted its naval blockade and guaranteed that it would not invade Cuba. Resenting his exclusion from the negotiations, Fidel Castro, the Cuban President, refused UNO entry, but by November the United States Defence Department was convinced that the weapons had been removed.

The world breathed a sigh of relief but the Cuban crisis had again reminded concerned people that peace was fragile and that a similar incident could spark off a global nuclear war. The Irish Government advised all its Departments, especially Civil Defence, to prepare a revised set of plans for consideration by the Internal Departmental Committee on Emergency Planning. These should be ready by December 31st 1962.

Could I phone my wife to come over? I always consult her on the choice of my clothes.'

PLANNING AND PARADING

Planning was to assume that:

1. A major world conflict could start with little or no advance warning.
2. It could be an all-out nuclear war from which biological or chemical warfare might develop.
3. Ireland could receive direct hits from nuclear devices or from conventional high explosive or incendiary bombs. These could be accidental or otherwise.
4. Fallout from nuclear attack on targets in the UK or elsewhere could reach any part of Ireland. This would be the most likely occurrence.

Meanwhile, Civil Defence was capturing public attention by parading, inviting prominent citizens to inspect exercises and by placing displays in shop windows. People were becoming attracted to its humane objectives. The organization was receiving plaudits from the media and from public representatives across the country. Its golden harp was playing a patriotic air and the public was responding.

THE 'CRASH PLAN'

The Department of Defence had prepared a draft newspaper article titled 'The Bomb and You'. It described what would happen in a nuclear war situation, explaining the 'deadly cloud' of fallout and methods of protection. It would be published as a desperate effort to warn the public in the absence of adequate notice of an impending nuclear strike. An October 1962 revision formed the basis of the *Householders' Manual*. It outlined a contingency procedure that became known as the 'Crash Plan'. The Plan required Local Authorities to establish protected Control Centres and equip them to become operational at short notice from March 31st 1963.

Government funding would cover seventy per cent of the cost. It would also contribute to developing Regional Centres and would purchase radiac instruments and five 'Green Goddess' fire fighting vehicles immediately (see Auxiliary Fire Service). Twenty more would follow over a period of time. Other purchases included thirty five ambulances and two Mobile Feeding Units.

In 1963, the Civil Defence School mailed a copy of *Bás Beatha* to every household in the country. Like the *Householder's Manual*, the illustrated booklet explained radioactive fallout and advised on warning systems and refuge areas for families and livestock. It brought snide asides from some who preferred to act like that feathered species with long necks whose heads and beaks crave sand!

FURTHER PLANNING

At the beginning of 1964, Civil Defence had a volunteer strength of about 12,300. By the end of the year the figure was 17,426. There were 170 training centres. Recruitment had been successful, but the 'Crash Plan' needed replacement.

The Secretary of the Department of Defence wrote to his counterpart in the Department of Finance concerning a new Civil Defence Plan 1965. He stated:

> It is essentially an administrative guide for Civil Defence development and will, of course, be subject to modification or alternation from time to time, in the light of any new ideas or knowledge as to planning for a war situation. Its purpose is the creation of a Civil Defence organization in which state departments, state-sponsored bodies, Local Authorities and public utilities will ultimately reach a state of preparedness which will ensure the best possible Civil Defence operational capability.

The Plan contained four inter-linked sections or phases that allowed for simultaneous reactions. Phase 1 assumed that the householder would have three days notice of fallout arrival. It placed the onus on Civil Defence for:

1. Warning of the arrival of fallout.
2. Advising the public to take precautionary measures as stipulated in *Bás Beatha*.
3. Notifying people as to when it would be safe to come out of the shelter in their homes.

Phase 2 provided for:

1. Improved warning to the public.
2. Better communications and reporting links.
3. More efficient arrangements at National Control.
4. Military assistance in monitoring the situation.

Phase 3 outlined an increased operational capacity for Civil Defence services. Combined and in broad terms, the first three phases allowed for development of preparations and maximum operational capability in a fallout situation without physical destruction.

Phase 4 outlined the use of all available resources in dealing with likely problems. It identified certain minimum requirements:

1. A blast protected permanent National Control Centre at a suitable distance from Dublin.
2. A Dispersal Plan for Dublin and Cork.
3. Communal fallout shelter arrangements.
4. A public warning system.
5. Regional Control Centres.
6. Operational bases and depots.

A400541 81

Members of the Monasterevin
Civil Defence Pipe Band, 1969

ACCOMMODATION AND WARNING

A communications room and canteen had been established in the Department of Defence Headquarters basement by 1965. Then the advantages of a National Control Headquarters outside the city became apparent. This led to consideration of Firmount House, County Kildare or the basement of a billet block in Custume Barracks, Athlone. By 1968, an interim decision on Athlone had been made (see Chapters 4 and 5).

The Civil Defence Branch at the Department of Defence prepared files on Refugee Accommodation and Dispersal Statistics. Local Authorities engaged in Dispersal Planning by categorizing schools, churches, hotels and other large institutions.

THE UNITED KINGDOM SCALES DOWN

In 1968, members of London's fashion-conscious élite were queuing to purchase from the Beatles' Apple boutique, a new £100,000 psychedelic store in the West End. The UK Government withdrew all funding towards Local Authorities' voluntary Civil Defence Service. They limited training to local officials and staffs of Government Departments. They retained Regional Operational Control in underground bunkers using information supplied from posts manned by Observer Corps personnel. Using tracking instruments, they would be capable of locating and quantifying bomb bursts. The Observer Corps would pass its data on to Local Authorities. An area receiving a nuclear strike would receive no assistance from Government. It would have to rely on its own peacetime emergency strategies in coping with destruction and radiation. The UK Government abandoned all training courses for volunteers and closed all their training schools with the exception of the Home Defence College at Easingwold, near York.

NORTHERN REFUGEES

Nuclear weapons had not been used in the Middle East 'Six Day' War (1967) or in the Vietnam War (1965-73). Yet, in the early 1970s their threat still affected relationships between world powers and international negotiations on limitation of weapon production began.

In Ireland, more pressing and immediate domestic problems were demanding the Government's full attention and the public's deep concern. The political turmoil in Northern Ireland prompted a Civil Defence circular of March 15th 1972 to warn: 'We could well be faced with the problem of having to cater for upwards of 50,000 homeless.'

Local Authorities received instructions to prepare for receiving refugees. Rural counties should expect at least 200 each, while Dublin and Cork should prepare for 2000 and 500, respectively. The border counties would provide transit facilities. Each Regional Civil Defence Officer (RCDO. See Chapter 4) would decide on distribution to counties.

BLOODY SUNDAY

Early in July 1971, Northern Ireland was enduring a confused mix of fact and rumour. Ulster Vanguard was claiming that a Protestant army of up to 70,000 was awaiting a mobilization call. 'Tartan Gangs', wearing plaid scarves to commemorate Scottish military victims, were running wild. The Twelfth of July Marches began as a young Catholic boy was shot dead in his home. Fear drove many mothers and fathers of families away from the turmoil. During August 9-10th, internment was introduced under Section 12 of the Special Powers Act.

Hundreds of refugees began moving out. Many of them arrived in Dublin. Civil Defence provided food for them at railway stations. On a particular day, Welfare volunteers served 1300 meals at Connolly Station alone. Some received accommodation in the city; others passed on to rural areas.

Army Field Hospitals at Finner Camp, Gormanston and Dundalk received Irish Red Cross Society and Civil Defence

Biddy White-Lennon, who played in the popular TV programme 'The Riordans' was also a member of Sutton Civil Defence Unit.

assistance, but Civil Defence cooperated in a number of capacities nation-wide. On the night of August 12th alone, 2,825 refugees reached Gormanston Camp. Ordinary householders pulled teddy bears, dolls and rocking horses out of attics and brought them to the camps. Clothing, television sets, games and books began piling up in stores of refugee centres, ready for allotment when families settled in.

The Welfare Service set up transit and rest-centres in Dundalk, Castleblaney, Sligo, Monaghan, Cavan and Omeath. Longford and Westmeath housed a large number of refugees and the Warden Service provided Information Posts in a number of locations. In time, all Civil Defence Regions became involved. At a peak period they were looking after 2,695 refugees. These were mainly in camps at Gormanston, Finner, Kilworth, Kildare, Kilkenny, Coolmoney and Tralee. The Garda Training Depot in Templemore catered for 600. Up to 2,714 were housed elsewhere – in colleges, schools, holiday camps and town halls. By mid-September, the refugees began returning and by Christmas only 200 remained, all in Kilworth Camp, County Cork.

In Derry, on January 30th 1972, thirteen people died as a result of an altercation between the British Army and Civil Rights marchers. The event became known as 'Bloody Sunday'. Fear of a recurrence in Newry on the following Sunday led to a well-planned operation involving all voluntary aid societies in County Louth. Civil Defence, supported by the Irish Red Cross Society, set up Casualty Collecting Points in Killeen and Omeath. A full Casualty unit from Dublin Civil Defence was on stand-by in Drogheda, but the main reserve was in Dundalk. Rescue and Warden Services attended and the Welfare Service provided meals. Order of Malta personnel from Dundalk, Ardee, Balbriggan, Navan and Drogheda attended. Irish Red Cross Society units came fully equipped with ambulances and sophisticated first aid equipment. Members of An Garda Síochána, the Defence Forces, Coras Iompair Éireann; nurses, doctors and student doctors arrived to volunteer assistance.

Personnel from Cavan Civil Defence came to Dundalk as observers and put a similar scheme into practice later when another Civil Rights march took place in Enniskillen. Their operational headquarters was in Bawnboy, covering approaches from across the border through Ballyconnell, Swanlinbar and Aghalane. Leitrim Civil Defence took responsibility for the mountain pass through Blacklion.

REVITALIZATION

Throughout the 1970s, the USSR entered a period of détente with the West. Ireland was focusing attention on the Northern Ireland situation, entry to the European Economic Union and escalating oil prices. The Civil Defence School's courses were concentrating more on refugee handling, on practical requirements for County Control staffs and on Warden, Welfare and Casualty training. The National Competitions became a highly popular feature of the decade, having evolved from similar informal events in the late 1960s. The rivalry was often intense. The series raised standards and whipped up considerable enthusiasm among participants and supporters. It also provided a valuable social and morale boosting outlet. A more ambitious concept was in the pipeline, however.

GROUND BURST IN WALES

An intensive recruitment drive for wardens formed part of hectic preparations preceding the first National Fallout Exercise that took place on October 24th 1976. It aimed at practising the Civil Defence network in a simulated fallout situation: It envisaged Nuclear Ground Bursts occurring in Wales and the North of England at 0610 hours. The yield in each case was one Megaton. Prevailing winds carried radioactive fallout to many parts of Ireland.

At once, it was a test of wardens, SIOs, communications and mobilization procedures. Everybody from Post Warden to National Control was involved. There were also links with the Meteorological Service, Irish Lights, An Garda Síochána, the Defence Forces, the Electricity Supply Board and Radio Telefís Éireann. The exercise attracted 2,382 wardens alone and was successful.

In Afghanistan the following year, a left-wing 'Armed Forces Revolutionary Council' overthrew the five-year-old republican regime of General Mohammad Daoud. During the last days of 1979, USSR forces moved into the country and installed Babrak Karmal as leader in its capital, Kabul. Hostilities between Iran and Iraq were reaching crisis point too. The voice of an environmental group called Greenpeace was beginning to receive attention. Its loudest call was against nuclear weapons.

STAR WARS AND WARDENS

The 1980s began with more tension in the Middle East. The US feared for its oil supplies in the region and began posturing. The Cold War again became a factor, its tensions increasing when President Reagan's administration planned to develop its Star Wars missile protection systems. The media, particularly television programmers, resurrected the horrific consequences of nuclear war that had filled pages and screens in the late 1950s and in the 1960s. Some Irish householders reacted by building domestic nuclear shelters but the majority of the population ignored the

Civil Defece School
Staff, 1982

reports and discussed the Derrynaflan chalice and other ecclesiastical objects discovered by metal-detector near Killenaule, County
Tipperary.

National Warden Exercises in those years made use of television in transmitting fallout information. An Garda Síochána,
Irish Lights and the Army Observer Corps participated.

Wardens had been using Avometers and Victoreens for measuring radiation since the early 1960s. They welcomed the issue of
a new instrument, called the ESS meter. The name derived from
a company at Shannon (Electro Mechanical System and Services)
that had manufactured it to Civil Defence School specifications.
The other services held National Competitions annually throughout this decade.

CHERNOBYL

On May 1st 1986, high radiation levels recorded in Scandinavia
caused grave concern. A few days later, USSR authorities admitted that there had been an explosion on April 26th at Number 4
Reactor of Chernobyl nuclear power station in the Ukraine and
that it had gone on fire. They also stated that the other three reactors had been closed down, that two people had been killed and
that 135,000 people had been evacuated from a thirty-five kilome-
ter zone.

A release of radioactive gases combined with dust affected

Civil Defence staff monitoring an oil tanker in Tarbert

adjacent regions of the USSR, and spread to many parts of Eastern and Northern Europe. Resulting long-term personal deformities have been disputed and assessments of the eventual death toll in cancer deaths linked with the catastrophe have varied from 8,000 to 80,000. Food produce had to be destroyed and rainfall on hills in Northern England and Wales affected grazing lands for sheep.

Air sampling at the Meteorological Office in Glasnevin, Dublin, seven days after the accident, indicated an increase in radiation level. Civil Defence personnel countrywide hastily began collecting samples of milk, vegetables and water. They sent these for testing to the Nuclear Energy Board (NEB) and to the Science faculty of University College Dublin. Results testified that water samples were clear and there was minor radiation in vegetables. Some milk samples were significantly high. Those from farms in Donegal caused real concern, but only for a few days. Readings over some weeks confirmed that radiation levels did not constitute a threat to health.

The incident caused a few ripples that were forgotten by a general public when a ten million pound art robbery took place at Russborough House, County Wicklow on May 21st and the Fianna Fáil leader, Charles Haughey T.D. opened officially Connaught Regional Airport at Knock, County Mayo on the 30th. There was concern among defence planners, however.

PEACETIME PLAN

Ireland, like many other countries, had not foreseen the local effects of an accidental crisis of this magnitude so the Government went about drawing up a Peacetime Nuclear Accident Plan. In March 1987, the Minister for Energy and Communications announced that a National Radiological Protection Institute of Ireland (RPII) would replace the NEB and would be the agency responsible for detecting and monitoring radioactivity. It would also study short and long term consequences of any other nuclear accident that might occur.

The first Radiation Course for Scientific Officers (SOs, formerly SIOs) took place in the Civil Defence School during April 1988. The SO's bailiwick now included low level radiation. Exercises helped to devise a methodology for extensive evacuation. Liaison with Local Authorities continued and the School distributed the more sophisticated Graetz Radiation Meters, recently purchased.

There was singing and dancing and flag waving in 1989 when the Berlin Wall came tumbling down signalling the end of the Cold War. Enthusiastic young people with sledge hammers assisted official demolition crews while souvenir hunters collected pieces of rubble and cheered at every breach; a welcome respite, but in February 1991 came the war involving the ejection of Iraq from Kuwait. The spread of conflict to involve nuclear powers again became a possibility.

The popular Civil Defence National Competitions ceased. A series of National Exercises in which members would work together rather than compete, replaced them.

Following the passage of the Radiological Protection Act, the Government established the RPII in 1991 and produced its Peacetime Plan in 1992.

'DOBRODOSLI' – BOSNIAN REFUGEES

In July 1992, the Irish Government decided to accept up to 200 people who had fled the fighting in Yugoslavia. Civil Defence personnel from Ratra House and some Dublin volunteers joined the Refugee Agency Board, members of the Irish Red Cross Society and others in an advance party that boarded two Aer Lingus flights for Vienna in the early hours of September 2nd. After landing, they met a group of Bosnian refugees of ages between 79 years and 22 days. Apprehensive, these unfortunate people boarded the planes. When the engines roared take-off and then reached cruising speed, each refugee received a card with a number allotting specific accommodation. One of the Civil Defence entourage described the emotion of the moment as realization dawned that they were really getting away from their hardship and would receive a welcome in a friendly country. This feeling of intense relief grew and when the captain announced the approach to

Dublin airport, there were moving expressions of relief and joy.

Meanwhile, Civil Defence volunteers back home rolled up sleeves and began washing and scrubbing the Nurses Home of Cherry Orchard Hospital, parts of which had not been used since the 1950s. Students on a Welfare course at Ratra House were pressed into service. Theirs was really 'hands on' instruction and some palms had welts when the building became habitable.

Volunteers had practised the Serbo-Croat word for welcome, 'Dobrodosli', and they used it with sincerity when the four Civil Defence forty-five-seat coaches rolled to a halt. Tired but relieved, the refugees alighted to enter their new temporary home. Broad smiles expressed their gratitude better than a thousand words.

Dublin Civil Defence handled the settling in process, but soon volunteers from all over the country were becoming involved on a rota system. Her Excellency Mary Robinson, Uachtarán na hÉireann, An Taoiseach, Albert Reynolds, T.D., and Minister of State at his Department, Noel Dempsey, T.D., visited. A seven-year-old Bosnian child, Amila Koro, presented flowers.

Civil Defence volunteers continued operating a general office and reception area and took on domestic management, security and assorted driving duties. There was little reward, save for the look of contentment in a child's eyes or the sight of a group of old women enjoying a pleasant chat. The 'Bosnian Refugee' situation was an uplifting experience for all involved. It was a prodigious expression of regard for the dignity and well-being of fellow men, women and children. Twenty years after the Northern refugee situation, Civil Defence members, particularly those in its Welfare and Warden services, were again giving solace and comfort to disturbed and distressed people.

Ireland's Celtic Tiger was then a mere cub. We were moving 'Towards 2000'. Yet, to older volunteers the Cherry Orchard experience was simply a global version of what they had experienced as children during World War Two – neighbourliness.

John Moriarty, A.C.D.O. Dublin with one of the senior guests

Top left:
Young Bosnian refugees settling in at Cherry Orchard, 1992

TOWARDS 2000

Feeding the homeless at
Grangegorman, 1992

There was gridlock in cities and towns. House building proliferated in villages within commuting distance of cities. The economy was booming and the Celtic Tiger was clawing its way to unprecedented prosperity. The end of a millennium was beckoning and the Cold War threat was diminishing. highjinksireland.com was becoming synonymous with fun and gaiety and fast life-style. U2 and *Riverdance*, in black glasses and blacker stockings were blazing musical trails around the world. Fallout from abroad was really dropping on Dublin's Temple Bar pavements – ejected stag-party-goers!

More soberly, Civil Defence policy was focusing on community support and emergency response. The 1992 development programme, Towards 2000, aimed at establishing structures and developing skills that would enable the organisation to face new challenges. It recognised that demands on resources would be at local or community level and would include responses to all sorts of requirements such as stewarding, environmental issues, flooding, blizzards, forest fires and search and recovery in river, lake and coastal areas.

In addition, the organization continued to broaden the scope of its rescue capability, streamline its evacuee reception arrangements and plan for radiological and other emergencies. Towards 2000 required all Local Authorities to implement provisions in line with local needs by the year 2000.

Humanitarian needs were beckoning again. For over a year that began in December 1992, the Defence Forces operated an emergency centre for the homeless of Dublin in a disused cinema in Unit J of St Brendan's Hospital, Grangegorman. From December 18th, Civil Defence served two meals each day. In all, 1,500 volunteers from around the country took part. They lived at Ratra House, prepared meals in kitchens set up in its syndicate rooms and delivered them to the centre. The Salvation Army eventually replaced the Defence Forces on December 21st 1993. Civil Defence personnel remained an extra day, helping the new-comers to initiate its feeding programme.

NATIONAL EMERGENCY PLAN

The nuclear threat still did not go away. Another plan of action, this time formulated by the Department of Energy, appeared in October 1992. Its booklet bore the title *National Emergency Plan for Nuclear Accidents*. It explained that the International Atomic Energy Agency (IAEA) had established a Convention on Early Notification of a Nuclear Accident and that the European Community had adopted a Decision on the Rapid Exchange of Information in the Event of a Nuclear Accident. Each of these, it said, would provide for early warning of an accident, for exchange of information and, in Ireland's case, for notifying the Communications Control Centre of An Garda Síochána. The Plan reiterated the need for training and equipping Civil Defence.

A member of the RPII would always be on the alert for any signal that might add another statistic to the catalogue of acci-dents and incidents at Sellafield (formerly Windscale), which incorporated the Thermal Oxide Reprocessing Plant of British Nuclear Fuel Ltd. (THORP). A major mishap at one of Britain's fourteen other power reactors would cause concern too. A Disaster Committee included representatives from An Garda Síochána, the Defence Forces, Civil Defence and the Metreological Service. It kept close contact with officials who bore responsibilities for Defence, Agriculture, Health, Environment, Marine, Transport, Energy and Communications.

MILLENNIUM – AND BEYOND

Part of the White Paper on Defence issued in April 2000 praised the efforts of Civil Defence over its fifty years in existence. It assured its future in three paragraphs:

> In the period 2000 to 2010, Civil Defence will continue to focus its efforts on enhancing its capacity to respond to emergencies as a high-quality second line service in addition to facilitating com-

of State, Civil Defence legislation will be updated to reflect the current and future roles of the organisation.

This work will be completed as soon as possible. The voluntary nature of the organisation will be preserved. There is a particular culture and ethos associated with voluntary activity which is widely recognised as being important in building community. This must be nurtured at all levels by continuing to build co-operative relationships with other service organisations but maintaining the distinctiveness of Civil Defence. The volunteer nature of the Civil Defence organisation gives each citizen the opportunity to serve his or her community and it is the public face of the delivery of local authority services at many events. The progress of the Better Local Government initiative of the Department of the Environment and Local Government highlights the importance of such factors.

The training provided to Civil Defence members will continue to be revised and updated in line with best practice throughout the emergency community. Co-ordinated training will be provided to support all needs. Efforts will continue to be made to increase the flexibility in delivery of Civil Defence training and advantage will be taken of the existence of the new opportunities provided by the electronic media, particularly the Internet. Liaison with third level institutions on collaborative programmes will continue.

The White Paper assured a continuation of a proud tradition. Civil Defence has endured criticism and praise during its fifty years of existence. Snide comment never daunted its leaders. Its members laughed off miscellaneous hardships as they carried out their tasks. These included hazardous assignments at scenes of major accidents that received press attention but also participation in rescue, first-aid, welfare and crowd-control duties at hundreds of less publicized incidents. At work or at play, competing or socializing, officers and volunteers enjoyed an enduring camaraderie. Underlying all was the knowledge that they were being patriotic in giving their time and energy to serving the community.

The Civil Defence School at Ratra House always displayed dedication and enthusiasm and imparted instruction with great skill and understanding. Its staff steered the Service through tense periods when the pressing of a button in a distant land might have brought disaster. Had that happened, they and the thousands they trained would have been heroes. As Johann Wolfgang von Goethe wrote in F*aust: Die Tat ist alles, nichts der Ruhm*: The deed is all, the glory nothing. In the knowledge that they realized and cared, brought awareness and persuaded, believed and prepared, past and present members of Civil Defence can celebrate the organization's Golden Jubilee with pride.

3

Reporting Progress

Cold facts provide the bones of any organization's story but a good helping of anecdote and extracts from contemporary journals, official documents and newspapers nourishes its flesh, allowing the historic outline to give way to less formal chronicling. The metamorphosis ensures that those who wish to look back now or many years later will sense the human side of fifty years of endeavour.

Recollections can never comprise a full overview. Civil Defence volunteers have participated in a variety of real and simulated situations over the years. These included stricken trawlers at sea, aircraft crashes in urban and remote rural areas, mountain rescues and searches for missing persons. They were often close to great tragedy, like during the search for bodies of drowned youths off Doolin, County Clare in August 1983. They spent some lively times too, and the Civil Defence uniform has been prominent at Circuit of Ireland Rallies, Saint Patrick's Day parades and Military Pilgrimages to Lourdes as well as at civic occasions in towns and cities all over Ireland.

As for Festivals! From the internationally famous to the Frogs in the Fens, few of the many across the land were without the support of the local Civil Defence volunteers. The selection of recollections that follows caught either the headlines or the fancy of a few storytellers.

IN THE BEGINNING

After the formal opening of the Civil Defence School at Ratra House, Phoenix Park on June 18th 1951 by the Minister for Defence, Oscar Traynor, T.D., the day's programme for the School's first course was:

Scales of Attack – Lt Col A.X. Lawlor
High Explosives and their Effects – W.J. Cotter B.E.
Administration – W.P. Blunden B.A.
Building Construction, Forms of Collapse, etc. – R.A.S. Crawford B.A. B.A.I.
Atomic Power (Film) – W.J. Cotter B.E.

On November 3rd 1952, Úachtarán na hÉireann, An tUasal Seán T.Ó Ceallaigh agus a bhean made the short journey to visit the new institution behind their back garden. The Attorney General accompanied them. He was to become a President too – Cearbhall Ó Dálaigh. Ministers present were Messrs Aiken (External Affairs), Ryan (Health), Derrig (Lands) and Traynor (Defence).

The Irish Times of March 3rd 1953 reported on the first women to undergo an Instructors Course at Ratra House: 'Two of the girls are officials of Cork Corporation, Miss Nancy Sammon, a native of County Mayo and Miss Claire Smith, from Cootehill, County Cavan. The third is Miss Sheila McCrann, a Dublin Corporation official and a native of Roscommon.'

EARLY RECRUITMENT

Volume 1, Number 1 of the *Civil Defence Bulletin* appeared in May 1957. Like five following issues, it was a simple, stencilled copy of typed text, the only adornment being the ringed harp badge of the organisation. Its editorial set out aims:

> The first issue of the *Civil Defence Bulletin* is presented with the hope that its regular circulation among you who helped to lay the foundations of the Civil Defence organisation will assist in solving your problems and maintain the keen interest in Civil Defence affairs that you have already shown.
>
> We believe that the bulletin should not be or become just another 'official channel'. We will try to keep you in touch with progress in Civil Defence at home and abroad. On the home front our efforts can only be successful if *you* let us have, from time to time, local Civil Defence news and views. We will welcome any suggestions or criticisms you may have to offer on the form or content of the bulletin and we will endeavour to meet the wishes of the majority.
>
> At this early stage and considering the interruption of a General Election it may be somewhat presumptuous to speak of 'progress'.
>
> We can, however, point with satisfaction to the opening of training classes in many counties and to numerous recruiting meetings.'

The magazine gave details of one meeting at Dublin's Mansion House and the enrolling of over 150 volunteers referred to in Chapter 2. It quoted portion of one of the rallying speeches:

> The Civil Defence Officer opened with an address in which he referred to the destructive powers of nuclear weapons. He stressed particularly the need for outside aid to stricken areas

after a nuclear attack and appealed to those who had shown suf-
ficient interest in Civil Defence to attend the meeting to complete the good work by enrolling in the organisation and attending classes. One of the general instructors followed with an illustrated talk on the comparative effects of the airborne weapons of
World War Two and modern nuclear weapons. Two films – *The
Atom Strikes* and *The H-Bomb* – concluded the meeting.

We are informed of another Civil Defence Officer who had
been working quietly for the past couple of years in factories,
business houses and sports groups in his area and found when
recruiting started that the volunteers from these sources preclud-
ed the necessity for public meetings. A third Civil Defence
Officer tells of very satisfactory results from a combination of
public meetings and a canvass in factories and business establishments.

We are not advocating any particular approach to recruiting.
What suits one area may not work at all in another. Local officials know best what will produce the best response in their own
areas. We do offer the suggestion that, where public response is
slow or unsatisfactory, ready-made classes might be forthcoming
as a result of a judicious approach to the local officials of such
organisations as the Red Cross, Order of Malta or St. John
Ambulance Brigade, Muintir na Tíre or the Irish Country-
women's Association. Some local branches of those bodies would
welcome the introduction of Civil Defence training as a means
of providing fresh interests for their members and many useful
recruits to Civil Defence could be obtained from them.

SUFFERING MOST

There was no issue of the Civil Defence journal between February
1958 and August 1960. Its reappearance with a more elaborate logo
reflected encouragement for the use of Irish in Government
departments that was popular at the time. *Irisleabhar na Cosanta
Sibhialta* was its new banner. Beneath it was a quotation from
Traolach Mac Suibhne (Terence Mac Swiney) when he succeeded the assassinated Tomás Mac Curtáin as Lord Mayor of Cork
on March 30th 1920: '... it is not they who can inflict most, but
they who can suffer most, will conquer.'

The speech of the Minister for Defence, Caoimhghín Ó
Beoláin, T.D., on the Estimate for Civil Defence for 1960-61
appeared in full. Portion of it read:

> While Civil Defence recruiting falls very much short of require-
> ments, it is nevertheless encouraging to find that, according to
> Local Authority returns, there was an increase in the last year of
> about 1,000 in the numbers who have joined Civil Defence. The
> total number of volunteers is now in the region of 4,800. In
> general, the Local Authorities recognize the need for more

volunteers and are doing their best to get them. My Department is likewise doing its part in having available the uniforms and equipment for many additional volunteers.

One of the gratifying features which is now becoming apparent in relation to the Civil Defence organization is that those who have joined are building up a useful nucleus in many towns throughout the country. Some of these groups are engaging in exercises and weekend camps and some counties are combining to carry out joint exercises. This is a heartening development and it shows, I believe, that the organization is now taking root and that we have a good foundation on which to build.

SMAOINTE AR OBAIR DHAONDHA

In November 1960, ten Irish soldiers on peacekeeping duties with the United Nations lost their lives in the Congo when Baluba warriors ambushed them.

Civil Defence provided crowd control at their funeral and a section marched in the cortege. A man who would become Civil Defence School Principal, Micheál Ó Gabhláin was looking on. He echoed the thoughts of the nation in a moving description of his own feelings, given in his native tongue:

Lá bríomhar geimhridh a bhí ann agus mé im' sheasamh i lár Sráid Uí Chonaill imeasc slua mhór dhaoine – bhi gach áit plódaithe agus bhíomar go léir ag feitheamh leis an rud céanna, sé sin teacht bródmhar, brónach ár naonúir saighdiúirí ar ais ón gCongo. Bhí atmosphéir an bháis 'san aer an lá úd agus cad 'na thaobh nach mbeadh nuair a chuimhnimid nach bhfuil ní is treise i n-dúchas nó sean-cuimhne na tíre seo ná omós don gníomh grod – go deimhin fadó ní dhearna na filí agus na scribhneóirí uile ach labhairt amach as líonmhaireacht an tréithe seo in ár sinnsear romhainn. Agus ón dtaobh sin, is léir a Ghaelí is atá an smaoineamh seo dúinne go léir.

Ach chun teacht ar ais don scéal, bhí codarsnacht mhór idir an lá seo agus an lá sin i lár Iúil nuair a chuadar amach go gealgháirtheach – ceiliúradh agus ceol á dtionlacan agus ilgnéitheacht agus foirfeacht chultúir dúchais ár gcine dá léiriú í bhfleá agus mórshiúl ómósach. Cinnte ag an am sin do chuaigh ár saighdiúirí amach cosúil leis na sean-mhisinéirí Éireannacha fadó a thug cúnamh agus chabhair do na daoine barbaireacha – ní raibh rudaí luachmhara in a n-aigeanta ach teachtaireacht an dóchais agus an spioraid, ach anois ba dhubhach dubhbhrónach a dteacht thar nais chugainn.

Ó mo áit, i lár Sráid Uí Chonaill, bhíos in ann na bannaí ceoil a chloisint, ceann amháin díobh ag seinnt marbh mairseál Chopin agus an ceann eile á thabhairt an mairseál clúmhar sin le Handel – 'Dead March in Saul' – ansan i ndeire na dála do chonacthas an chéad-bhanna cheoil ón Arm ag teacht go mall réidh, brónach – ina dhiaidh sin do tháinig na sluaite ilgnéitheacha aonaid ón Arm agus ón tSeirbhís Cabhlaigh agus daoine eile ó buíonta sibhialta agus ón bhFórsa Cosanta Áitiúil.

Díreach ina ndiaidh sin go léir do tháinig buíon speisialta dhúinne. Buíon na gCosanta Sibhialta a bhí tofa, idir fir agus mná ón eagraíocht anseo againnse i mBaile Átha Cliath. Agus nárbh dheas iad na fir agus na mná sin agus iad gléasta ina gculaith gorma agus ainm na seirbhísí go léir scríobhtha ar a gcaipín agus ar a ngualainn. Bhíodar go léir ann: múchadh tóiteán, bárdaigh agus gach uile. Ach ina dhiaidh sin arís do chonaic mé banna eile ag teacht agus díreach ina dhiaidh sin do bhí na lorraí le cónraí na marbh – gach cónra clúdaithe le brat na hÉireann agus brat na Náisiún Aontaithe – iad á leirú árd-thréithe an bhorraidh agus an fháis thar cuimse faoi ghluaiseacht na cirte agus na síochána a bhí sáite ionnainne go léir nuair a chualamar an scéal ar dtúis.

Nuair do chonaic mé féin an radharc san, ní raibh na deora i bhfad ó mo shúile agus ag féachaint síos na sráide dhom do thugas faoi ndeara an bhuíon sin againne ón gCosaint Sibhialta. Ansan ní rabhas in ann ach cuimhneamh ar na cosúlachtaí a bhí idir na saighdiúirí marbha seo agus gach uile saoránach atá in eagraíocht Chosant Sibhialta an lae inniú. An obair atá idir láimhibh ag an gCosaint Shibhialta is cosúil í le'n obair atá á dhéanamh ag na saighdiúirí san gCongo. Daoine óga cumasacha ag dul imbun oibre ar son na síochána agus ar son leasa an chine daonna go ginearálta, iad go léir.

Agus anseo sa bhaile, ní taise do shaoránaigh na Cosanta Sibhialta an smaoineamh seo – sprid na hiomaíochta ag dul i ngéire dionnta go léir, spéis an phobail dá mhúsailt agus comharthaí fáis agus nirt agus tuar dóchais don náisiún go léir. Cosúil lenár saighdiúirí san gCongo más rud é go dtuitfidh lá na coise tinne – i bhfad uainn an tolc – beidh an Chosaint Shibhialta i láthair againn chun an obair dhaonna do leanúint agus do thabhairt chun deagh-chríche.

Ansan, taobh istigh de dheich nóiméad bhí na cónraí imithe agus an fhad is a bhíos ag féachaint orthu ag imeacht i dtreo na Cearnóige Pharnell do bhí na smaoinmte agus na pictúirí thuas léirithe im' aigne. Ach anois bhí an slua mhór ag imeacht agus cuma an bhróin orthu go léir. Ansin bhí a fhios agam go raibh am m'imeachta tagaithe. Mar sin do thosaigh mé ag dul i dtreo na hoifige – mé fhéin agus mo smaointe brónacha.

PARADES AND PROGNOSTICATIONS

The sixth issue of *Irisleabhar*, dated September 1961, took on a stapled magazine format. Now printed on good quality gloss paper, it still bore the MacSwiney quotation. The front cover carried a photograph showing Uachtarán na hÉireann, Eamonn De Valera taking the salute from a well turned out group of Civil Defence female volunteers. They were passing Dublin's historic General Post Office during the 1960 Easter Parade (see photograph page 6).

Underneath, in bold print, an old Irish saying warned: 'Ní hé lá na gaoithe lá na scolb' or 'The windy day is not the day for scollops.' Scollops were loose sticks for securing thatch and no sensible thatcher would risk having to work on a windy day. So the civil population was receiving warning to take time by the forelock and avoid losing the chance to prepare.

The Minister for Defence was obviously aware of some criticism about preparing for what many thought would never happen. In his Dáil speech on the Estimate for Civil Defence that year, he said:

> We, in this country, are in the very fortunate position of being able to hold whatever views we wish and, within the law, to express those views. We recognise that views on Civil Defence other than ours are prevalent in some circles – very often amongst those who set themselves up to be the champions of world peace. It is doubtful, however, if the individuals concerned have taken the trouble to study this whole question, in all its complications, in the same detailed and prolonged way as An Roinn Cosanta has been doing over the years.
>
> Our studies have led us to the unshakeable belief that Civil Defence is well worth while. That we are not alone in this belief is evidenced by the fact that the principles of Civil Defence have been accepted by the governments of many countries, including Algeria, Australia, Austria, Belgium, Bulgaria, Canada, Czechoslovakia, Denmark, Egypt, Finland, France, West and East Germany, Great Britain, Greece, Italy, Japan, Netherlands, Norway, Pakistan, Philippines, Spain, Switzerland, Turkey, USA, USSR.
>
> This is an impressive list that should convince any reasonable person that Civil Defence is not worthless. In my opinion, it also includes sufficient 'uncommitted countries' to dispel any idea that Civil Defence is merely a device to 'condition' people in certain countries to accept the fact that they themselves may have to resort to the use of nuclear weapons.

OBSERVER CORPS, HUNGER AND COWS!

The year 1961 saw the establishment of an Army Observer Corps to provide a radiation warning and monitoring service in the event of nuclear war. Also, eight Permanent Defence Force Commandants were seconded to the Civil Defence Branch to become Regional Civil Defence Officers. (See Chapters 2 and 4) The Minister was aware of a feeling among some Civil Defence volunteers that the Defence Forces might usurp their function.

He and others were at pains to assuage fears. They pointed out that army officers assisted the ARP organisation during World War Two, yet air raid precautions were not military functions.

In April 1962, there were initiatives to assist the Freedom from Hunger Campaign that had been established in 1945 by the Food and Agriculture Organisation of the United Nations Organisation. It aimed at helping nations to combat hunger and malnutrition. A National Collection organised by the Irish Red Cross Society received considerable assistance from Civil Defence volunteers.

CUBAN CRISIS

In September 1962, the *Irisleabhar* took on the blue jacket that was to last, with a few minor alterations in style, for many years. The issue reported a significant increase in training centres throughout the country.

The Cuban crisis was on everybody's lips. Many years after it, on April 19th 1999, Gene Kerrigan wrote in the *Sunday Independent* about his feelings at the time. His headline was 'Learning To Love The Bomb' and part of his tongue-in-cheek article went:

> In the grounds of St Finbar's national school we talked about the Cuban missile crisis. Kevin Grogan, Brendan Brady and me. I said that when the war started we could look up and see the missiles passing over us. The American ones would come from the Broombridge Road direction, on their way to Russia; the Russian ones would come from the direction of Phibsboro, on their way to the USA. We'd just have to look up – I looked up – and we'd see them passing, right up there.

FLEADH CEÓIL

Comhaltas Ceolteóirí Éireann brought its annual Fleadh Ceóil to its place of origin, Mullingar, during the Whit week-end of 1963. The occasion was marred by excessive drinking and dangerous bottle-throwing and the poet John Montague (*The Rough Field*. Mountrath 1972) later recorded:

> There were two sounds, the breaking
> Of glass, and the background pulse
> Of music. Young girls roamed the streets with eager faces,
> Pushing for men. Bottles in hand, they rowed out for a song:
> *Puritan Ireland's dead and gone,*
> *A myth of O'Connor and O Faoláin.*

Over 500 members of Civil Defence from all over the Midlands participated in the Fleadh. The organization's close colleagues from Tullamore, the Order of Malta Cadets' Band, led the impressive group in the opening parade. There were no reports of volunteers being involved in a mock dirge for Pope John XXIII that took place when he died during the event, on June 3rd. Perhaps they were among those of whom, Montague wrote:

> In the early morning the lovers
> Lay on both sides of the canal
> Listening on Sony transistors
> To the agony of Pope John.

PRESIDENTS, PLOUGHING AND PENTONVILLE

Later that month, Civil Defence supplied Welfare Service personnel, a canteen and other equipment for feeding extra Gardai drafted into Dublin. President John F. Kennedy had come to visit. Volunteers were on duty in other locations too, during those eventful days from June 26th to 29th.

Civil Defence had 12,300 volunteers and 170 training centres at the beginning of 1964. Later in the year, the Irish Red Cross Society and the Ambulance Corps of the Order of Malta reached substantial agreement with the Department of Defence regarding the roles of their respective organisations in Civil Defence policy. Wearing their own distinctive uniforms, recruited and trained independently by their own officers, they would constitute elements of the Civil Defence Casualty Service.

A Civil Defence Post Warden, Charles Keegan from Enniskerry, County Wicklow, won the World Ploughing Championship in Vienna in 1964. At a reception to honour the achievement, Paddy O'Reilly sang a self-composed ballad eulogising 'The Post Warden from Ballinagee.' Publication of the song in *Irisleabhar* was promised but it did not appear. Censorship?

An impressive cover picture on the April 1965 issue showed a representative detachment of Civil Defence volunteers from the Dublin area forming a Guard of Honour at the state funeral for the return of the remains of Roger Casement for re-interment on March 1st. The patriot had been hanged in Pentonville Prison, London on August 3rd 1916. The charge was high treason, in attempting to import arms for the Easter Week Rebellion.

ARMOUR AND COMPLIMENTS FLYING

The Fiftieth Anniversary of the Easter Week Rebellion was celebrated in a number of venues and in a variety of forms. An elaborate pageant called *Aiséiri*, directed by Tomás Mac Anna was a major feature. It took place in Croke Park. The theme was republicanism and rebellion in Ireland before and during Easter Week 1916.

State funeral of Sir Roger Casement

Below:

Actor, Jim Norton, surrounded by admiring group of Dublin Welfare personnel at *Aiséirí* pageant – Croke Park

A section of the Auxiliary Fire Service had a Green Goddess in attendance, with a line of hose laid along the upper tiers of the Hogan Stand. The Welfare Service fed 500 people including Padraic Pearse (Ray McAnally) Robert Emmett (Jim Norton) and James Connolly (Joe Lynch) each night. Mícheál macLiammóir was the Voice of History and he joined the Minister for Defence and other dignitaries who sampled CDC (Civil Defence Cuisine!) after performances.

One alert Civil Defence volunteer noticed a ragged looking 'tramp' lurking near the actors' dressing area during the opening performance. He reported the matter to a Military Policeman who duly set about ejecting the intruder. Tomás MacAnna had to come to the rescue and explain that the 'tramp' was the comedian, Cecil Sheridan, dressed and ready for some looting in O'Connell Street.

Snow, hail and storm marred the occasion and a Cork volunteer narrowly missed being hit by a flying armoured car that blew away from Bob Head's splendid set on the pitch and landed on Hill 16.

The *Cork Examiner* of July 13th carried an example of the type of letter that appeared all over the country from time to time, praising the efforts of Civil Defence:

Sir,
I wish here to extend a token of my appreciation to the entire Cork Civil Defence and to four of its members in particular: Sub-Officer Richard Walsh and Fireman Brian Bolster of the Cork Fire Brigade, Willie Sheehan of C.I.E. and a Nurse Dignam.

While on a visit to Ireland last month I was involved in an automobile accident at Monadrishane, County Cork. My wife, three children and my brother were in the car which overturned in a field after having been hit from behind by another car. The Civil Defence personnel, returning from an exercise at Kilworth, were immediately on the scene and took instant command of the situation. Together with a doctor who was unknown to me, they rendered moral and first aid in a manner which reaps great credit upon themselves and upon Civil Defence.

I can do no more than say that these people conducted themselves above and beyond the call of duty and on behalf of my family I wish to extend our sincere thanks to them.

We would appreciate if you could see fit to publish this letter in the *Cork Examiner* so that the people of Cork may be afforded an opportunity to become more cognizant and proud of their Civil Defence Force.

Michael J. Corcoran
95-17 41st Avenue, Elmburst, N.Y. 11373

Dublin Civil Defence participating in 1916 Commemoration Parade on Easter Sunday, 1966

GOOD TIMES AND BAD

In 1967, the Civil Defence Officers Association of Britain organised an Educational Cruise from Tilbury Docks on the Thames. Two Irish Civil Defence members answered an invitation to sail. They visited places like Guernsey, Gibraltar, Tangier and Lisbon. Nine pence for gin, ten pence for whiskey and a Roman Catholic Chaplain's dispensation from abstaining from meat on Fridays – what could be better? At the nightly discothèque, assorted foreign revellers kept calling for the 'Irish Dance' demonstrated ably by the Civil Defence cruisers. It was not 'The Walls of Limerick', but Brendan Bowyer's 'Hucklebuck'! At Gibraltar's St Michael's Cave, monkeys collected the entrance fee. Just like some places at home!

Doctor Miriam Hederman, a regular broadcaster and commentator of the period, contributed some enthusiastic comment about Civil Defence to a number of issues of *Irisleabhar*. In April, 1968 she said:

> Members of Civil Defence know their neighbourhood and their neighbours and are themselves known. They know alternative routes if main roads are cut; they know what to do if electric supplies fail or lines of communication are out of commission. Ideally, they are self-reliant and trained to cope. Normally they

Mobile Feeding Unit at
Civil Defence Exhibition in
Cork 1968

are less likely to lose their heads than if they never received any such training. Surely it is in the interest of local authority, at all levels, to see that there is a cadre of such people in its community and that they have at least the minimum amount of equipment to help everyone in an emergency? This is the least we might expect from those who proclaim that they have our interest at heart and that they exist only to serve us, the people, the potential victims, the possible survivors.

The same issue carried an extract from the German Civil Defence Bulletin *Zivilschuts*. It outlined the type of operations that took place in Vietnam and stressed the importance of Civil Defence training in the development of initiative and utilization of quite primitive methods of protection in warfare.

More and more instances of Civil Defence assistance to victims of accidents were receiving reportage in national and local press. In November 1968, for example, a single-engine aircraft on a flight from the Isle of Wight to Shannon crashed in the mountains of Cappaghwhite, north of Tipperary. The pilot was killed and Rescue and Casualty units from Limerick were on the scene to assist at the removal of the remains.

In January 1969, snow trapped a bus on a bog road at Calary, County Wicklow. A Green Goddess and crew from Bray rescued the female passengers. The men had to settle for a County

Council truck! Just two weeks later, unprecedented high tides crashed across Bray promenade. Civil Defence Volunteers were active, sandbagging houses on the sea-front.

The Casualty Service in Clones, County Monaghan claimed to be the first to have a trained religious section when two groups of nuns, one from the St Louis Convent and another from the Sacred Heart Convent, completed courses.

IN THE CAN

The television programmes 'One Man and his Dog' and 'Bracken' come to mind when recalling the shooting of the Civil Defence instructional film, *Dangerous Dust*. The crew shot many of the location scenes around the farm of District Warden Pat Nolan, Ballymurrin, Kilbride, County Wicklow. Pat's farm assistant, Post Warden Liam Hamilton, appeared in the film even though his wife had just given birth before the shooting of his scene began.

The farm animals were not so obliging. The segment of the film outlining protection of livestock from fall-out involved getting sheep into a stable. Inside, a small camera crew awaited their entrance. Actor Cecil Sheehan played the farmer and, try as he would, he could not get the sheep to oblige. Take after take produced similar results. No Wicklow sheep ever went into a stable, particularly one with strange men and suspicious-looking contraptions inside.

Pat Nolan had an idea. He opened another door at the back of the stable, removed the camera crew and led one sheep through the building. As sheep do, the others followed. Pat kept up this rehearsal, allowing in one of the crew at a time. There was one minor mishap, when a sheep upturned the cameraman, but the flock gradually became used to the procedure and the scene was in the can in two shakes of a ram's tail!

After its premiere in Griffith Barracks, Dublin on November 30th 1970, *Dangerous Dust* became popular when screened at centres nation-wide. Some say a handsome ram was nominated for an Oscar!

DECIMALS AND DESIGN

Civil Defence prepared for Decimalization Day that arrived on February 15th 1971. The January issue of *Irisleabhar* ran a four page feature, with illustrations about the new currency and how it would affect assorted transactions. The instructions were in the Irish language, *ach thuith an phingin le gach duine!*

The first design alteration in ten years adorned *Irisleabhar na Cosanta Sibhialta* in July 1971. Its banner simply read *Cosaint*

Shibhialta with *Civil Defence Journal* vertically beneath and to the left of the familiar jacket photograph. The basic colour was green, but this would change to pink or blue or orange in following issues. The Terence MacSwiney quotation disappeared.

REFUGEE STATUS!

The Northern Ireland refugee situation produced an occasional amusing anecdote. Refugees often arrived in good spirits initially but tended to become depressed after a few days. An incident occurred in a town where they had quarters in a local hospital. A strict warden was patrolling its grounds after dark. In a shrubbery, he discovered a young man and woman in what adults of those days called a 'compromising position'. The warden, a clean-living bachelor, was horrified and delivered a homily on morals to the couple before ordering them indoors.

Furious, they gathered the remainder of the refugees together and enlisted their support for a gesture of protest. They decided to seek accommodation elsewhere and thought the local army barracks might be more tolerant towards amorous adventure. They realized, however, that beds might not be readily available on their midnight arrival and so they marched boldly through the streets of the town, each carrying a pillow.

The barracks stood about three miles from the hospital and they grew tired now and then and used their pillows to rest on the footpath – or adopt other hasty compromising positions.

The Barrack Orderly Officer was no less strict than their warden. He turned them away. There was no room on the inside – even for refugees with pillows. So the long trek back began. There are some who say that, when they told the warden of their being refused entry to the barracks, he uttered the dreadful pun: 'That was a bitter pillow to swallow.'

After a few days, some of the younger people from Derry missed the stone-throwing escapades they had been enjoying at home. A bull occupied a paddock in the hospital farm. The youths collected pieces of rock and waited behind a ditch until the animal came close enough to present a good profile of its well-proportioned endowment. They opened fire and scored something the opposite to a bulls-eye that hurt far more! The unfortunate beast sped around the enclosure uttering mighty bellows that could be heard a mile away.

The late Dublin Assistant County Welfare Officer Syl FitzPatrick was controller of a refugee centre at the Royal Dublin Society's show grounds at Ballsbridge, Dublin. He once recalled refugees who arrived from Gormanston, where their main concern was the care of their children. 'By the time they reached the RDS, the first false elation had gone and the full significance of

Refugees arriving at St Stephen's Hospital, Sarsfieldscourt, Cork, 1972

lost homes and lost possessions had begun to sink in,' he said. He remembered refugees' depression and the nuns at Donnybrook Convent who provided bathing and washing facilities. This was of immense importance, considering 'how the women had just grabbed their children and run,' he said.

Syl also remembered trips to Sandymount strand, and the Dun Laoghaire branch of Rotary Club of Dublin organizing outings to Dublin Zoo, the Metropole Cinema and to John B. Keane's *Big Maggie* at the Gas Company Theatre. He mentioned too the kindness of Tallaght Community Centre, The Red Cross Society of Ireland, the Irish Girl Guides. Pleasant surprises from individuals ranged from a home made cake for the staff to 'taking out mothers and children for tea'.

UNIFORMS

A Sub Officer of the Auxiliary Fire Service contributed a courageous article to *Cosaint Sibhialta* in April 1972. It criticized the Civil Defence uniform. Bill Stewart made his points with some humour. About assorted colours in lanyards he wrote, 'Let them be colourful, but don't end up as if the wearer was a Flag-Lieutenant in a fictional navy.' He was no less critical of flashes, saying, 'Remember they are worn on a uniform, not a hitch-hiker's bag.'

'– and a suitable skirt for the ladies, of course!'

Members of Monaghan AFS at the scene of the bomb explosion in Monaghan town on May 17th, 1974

During the night of April 18th-19th 1974, members of the Warden and Casualty Services of Dublin Civil Defence who lived in Ballymun donned their uniforms and assisted the evacuation of residents from a block of flats. A serious fire had broken out in the basement. While moving residents to Ballymun Comprehensive School, the volunteers were alerting the Welfare and Rescue Services. A local supermarket supplied provisions and Welfare volunteers prepared meals and beds. In the event, by 0230 hours the building was considered safe and the well-fed residents returned to their own beds.

One old man may have been in a time warp. He did not recognize the uniforms and asked, 'Are youze the LSF or wha'?'.

DUBLIN AND MONAGHAN BOMBS

Older Dubliners were recalling the ARP at the North Strand bombing as they watched Civil Defence personnel in action on May 17th 1974. Three car bombs exploded almost simultaneously during the evening rush hour, at 5.30 p.m. There was one was in Talbot Street and another in South Leinster Street off Nassau Street and beside Trinity College. The third was in Parnell Street. The Talbot Street bomb killed twenty-five and injured 100 people.

Scenes of destruction in the aftermath of the Monaghan bombing

Less than ninety minutes later, Monaghan Auxiliary Fire Service was at the scene of a bombing in its home town and cooperated with the Regular Fire Brigade. A Casualty section assisted the injured and expedited the removal to hospital of serious cases. The Civil Defence ambulance came from Clones as a reserve vehicle. Six people died as a result of the explosion.

BURST BANKS, BLAZES AND BOMBS

'The Auld Triangle Went Jingle-Jangle' in Tullamore on August 4th 1974. It was not the Royal Canal, however, but the Grand Canal that caused a Red-Alert. It had burst its banks at Killeen, near Daingean. A sixty-foot breach was threatening human life and livestock as water gushed through, flooding the surrounding area. Offaly Civil Defence joined with Order of Malta units from Tullamore in assisting evacuation of families. A group of twenty Rescue personnel built a dam to divert the water to a nearby stream.

Water was a problem in Bandon, County Cork too. A tributary of the Bandon River had burst its banks and the town experienced severe flooding. Rescue vehicles towed cars to high ground and the Auxiliary Fire Service pumped water from homes. Civil Defence volunteers from Youghal, Carrigaline and Shanbally joined local colleagues in the operation.

There had been considerable flooding at the Post Office and Telephone Exchange and the Minister for Posts and Telegraphs, Conor Cruise O'Brien T.D., later offered congratulations for Civil Defence assistance.

The Wicklow Auxiliary Fire Service saw action at the disastrous fire that destroyed the magnificent Powerscourt House, Enniskerry on the night of November 4th-5th 1974. It assisted regular brigades from Greystones, Wicklow, Rathdrum and Bray.

A car bomb exploded outside Kay's Tavern, Dundalk on December 19th. Rescue teams came from Dunleer and Collon to join the local unit. Casualty, Welfare and Rescue units, including some from Drogheda, stood by at Louth County Hospital in case of further explosions.

The year ended with Wexford volunteers in action at a place with a stirring history of action in the 1798 Rebellion. Post Warden Chris Hill of Tubberneering tried to warn a train of an obstruction on the line at Clough, near Gorey, but could not prevent a serious crash. A Rescue team helped clear debris throughout the afternoon and evening. Personnel from other services offered their services also, but were not required. The Chairman and Board of

A 'casualty' from Cork City Civil Defence deep inside a cave during an exercise

Córas Iompair Éireann later complimented Civil Defence for its response and 'unselfish dedication'.

Enlarged photographs of Civil Defence in action at all the year's disasters were on display at the organisation's stand at the 1976 Spring Show. The episodes were to continue. A car bomb exploded outside the Three Star Inn in Castleblaney on March 7th. One man died and seventeen people received injuries. The local Casualty Service rendered first aid. An accidental explosion occurred on the *M.V. Rathowen* at Verolme dockyard on August 23rd. It force hurled upwards some men who were working below deck, ejecting them through a manhole. One became entangled in a rope fifty feet above. This broke his fall and probably saved his life. The Killeagh-Youghal Rescue Unit gave assistance.

TIES AND THINGS

During 1976, in navy blue or dark brown, the Civil Defence School polyester tie became available, post free, at £2.00. Its motif, recalling the School's location, was a pale blue Phoenix. A yellow stripe recognised the international colour symbol for radioactivity. Before the cold days of winter arrived, scarves and head-scarves with similar design, went on the market.

On June 15th, some Westport volunteers were hoping for an early night before sitting for their Leaving Certificate Examinations next morning. Instead, they spent the night on Croagh Patrick searching for a thirteen-year-old American tourist. A mobilization order was issued at 2200 hours and volunteers joined local civilians, members of An Garda Síochána and of the Order of Malta in combing the northern and southern slopes of the mountain.

The searchers discovered the unconscious boy in an area known as The Cone. By radio, they reported his condition to a doctor who instructed that the boy should not be removed without first receiving medical attention.

This was administered before midnight. Through heavy cloud and darkness, using flares, volunteers had to carry the lad over extremely difficult terrain to the recognised Pilgrims' Path and, later, to safety in Castlebar Hospital.

Some of the civilians taking part in the operation failed to return to base and a second search became necessary. The story had a happy ending and everybody prayed to St Patrick that the student volunteers would fare well in their examinations.

Clare Civil Defence Rescue Service received congratulations from *Aer Rianta* for assisting at a 1976 aircraft accident at Shannon in which five people lost their lives.

One of the biggest fires ever experienced in Limerick City occurred on January 5th 1977 at Rank's Mill on Dock Road. The AFS succeeded in its allotted task of preventing the blaze from reaching a large silo, considered to be a dangerous flash point.

Nine days later, during a severe snow and hail storm, Wicklow Civil Defence conducted search and rescue operations in the mountains near Roundwood. The episode continued for three days.

That year ended with a worthy environmental exercise as volunteers patrolled coastal regions tending to and collecting statistics on seabirds that were oiled or beached for other reasons. New roles for Civil Defence in the future were becoming apparent. *Cosaint Shibhialta* was taking occasional flights and landings of fantasy. An imaginative feature titled 'Take Me To Your Leader' By E.A. Farrell began:

> Miniolimpic has landed in his flying saucer. He has travelled through space to reach planet OKT 427 or Earth as we usually call it. He is the commander of his spacecraft and he is justifiably proud of the way his crew and himself have successfully concluded this long and arduous journey.
>
> He knows, however, that he cannot now take it easy. He must make contact with the natives of this planet and he must make sure that his crew does not relax and get careless – who knows what danger there may be from these extraordinary earthlings?
>
> Using a well-known intergalactic sign language, Miniolimpic

Display of inflatable tent at Ratra House

says, 'Take me to your leader'. He adopts a friendly attitude but still lets everyone know that he is no slob. As luck would have it, there was a District Warden in the group of earth people. He took command of the situation and made the visiting Ratrans feel welcome. This was the start of a long friendship between Miniolimpic and Mr Origin, the District Warden.

SYNTAX FOR SMILES

From a *Cosaint Shibhialta* feature offering hints on safety in the home, came this gem about things to note in the bathroom: '...make a regular check on the proper functioning of your equipment...'

Reportage on the Auxiliary Fire Service National Competition on June 10 1978 told how 'A charming member of the Dunleer Ladies team, Josephine McKeown, was the choice of Mary Rose O'Donnell and Eddie Dunne, as Miss Flame 1978.

Mayo County Council's County Control was in trouble. Built before Health Boards were established, it was under a maternity section of Castlebar Hospital and in 1978 people began claiming that this contravened the Geneva Convention. The *mother* of all rows ended with re-location of the centre to an area beneath the Municipal Offices.

The Papal visit provided Civil Defence with an opportunity to demonstrate its effectiveness in serving the community in peacetime

Because of their expertise and civic spirit, volunteers often responded to human tragedy, even when not formally called out. The reception and care of 216 Vietnamese 'Boat People' in August 1979 was one example. The following month, His Holiness Pope John Paul II visited Ireland. A major involvement of Civil Defence demands a detailed account.

PAPAL VISIT

The Papal visit provided Civil Defence with an unusual and unexpected opportunity to demonstrate its effectiveness in serving the community in peacetime. In all, up to 6,500 volunteers became involved. They undertook a variety of tasks.

In most instances more than the numbers required were available for assorted duties. They endured hardships willingly and displayed initiative in coping with the demands of the occasion. Their general bearing and conduct elicited warm praise. Expressions of thanks reached the Department of Defence from ecclesiastical and civil authorities.

From Number One Region, 130 volunteers participated. Twenty were from Cork City, nineteen from Cork North, twenty-one from Cork South, thirty from Cork West and forty from Kerry.

Number Two Region's total was 555. Limerick City provided 115 and Limerick County 200. Eighty came from North Tipperary and 160 from Clare.

Number Three Region provided 125 from Galway city where the Pope said his Mass for Youth. Bad weather made things difficult for volunteers at Knock. There, 350 Mayo volunteers and 185 from Roscommon attended. The region's total was 660.

Number Four Region was also involved at Knock. Donegal provided 140, Leitrim 201 and Sligo 115, bringing the total to 456.

Due to its central position, Number Five Region supplied volunteers to the Phoenix Park, Knock, Clonmacnois and Galway. From its total of 491, Laois, Offaly, Westmeath and Longford provided 183,108,100 and 100 respectively.

Approximately 400 members of Civil Defence from Number Six Region officiated at the Papal visit to Drogheda. The Casualty Service provided 140, Welfare had thirty and 230 from the other Services carried out stewarding duties.

Number Seven Region carried out the mammoth tasks associated with the Phoenix Park and Maynooth visits. Duties included stewarding, first aid, welfare and other tasks.

The contribution by counties for the Phoenix Park venue was: Dublin, 920; Wicklow, 160; Meath, 210 and Kildare, fifty. Another 150 volunteers from County Kildare were on duty in Maynooth. Personnel from Number Eight Region (attached to Number Seven for the operation) totalled 270. In all, the region organised and deployed a force of 1,760.

Although far away from the main areas of action, a further 273 volunteers from Number Eight Region travelled to different locations. Wexford sent forty-three; Carlow twenty-eight; Kilkenny, twenty; Waterford County, fifty-eight; Waterford City, sixty-one; Tipperary South Riding, sixty-three.

NATIONAL EXERCISE

In *Cosaint Shibhialta* of January 1980, Micheál Ó Gabhláin made some telling points about turning a blind eye to possible dangers. He concluded his article by remarking, 'There is no doubt that we do lose sight of our objectives... Civil Defence is a bit like the hens from Mayo. Now and again we see our aims clearly and set out with great enthusiasm to achieve them. But by degrees we get immersed in the daily scratch and scrape. And so the day wears on and the night approaches – the night when no man can work.'

Then he went on to explain his reference to Mayo hens. A scrap of the county's folklore wisely states:

> All the hens around here came in the beginning from Scotland, and they are always trying to get back there. Every morning they set out to go back to Scotland, but then they start scratching and pecking and they forget their intentions. By nightfall they have forgotten all about Scotland.

(Could the Mayo people have been talking about some past Irish Rugby teams?)

While many people were sleeping on Sunday morning, March 30th 1980, the Communications Officer of Civil Defence introduced the National Fallout Exercise on Radio Telefís Éireann. Networks 1 and 2 carried 'Network 80'and its fiction of international tension leading to nuclear bomb bursts on England. The appearance of Commandant Gerry Newman on living room screens was adding drama and a sense of involvement that had been missing in previous exercises. People who watched were realising what Civil Defence was really about.

Concentrated press coverage followed, and carried the same message: this concerns everybody, folks. RTE's 'Week Out' programme and Radio 2's 'Kenny Report' interviewed Civil Defence personnel. BBC Northern Ireland's 'Good Morning Ulster' radio programme interviewed the Director of Civil Defence, Gerry Scully.

At Ratra House, on March 28th, there was a formal hand-over of twelve seventeen seater mini-buses adapted for carrying standard Civil Defence equipment. The Personnel and Equipment Vehicles (PEVs) were intended primarily for Rescue Service use but would be available for training and assorted operational needs.

MORE DISASTERS

A unit from Cork North Rescue Service assisted at the Buttevant Rail Disaster on August 1st 1980. Eighteen passengers died and seventy-five received injuries. Casualty personnel stood prepared also, but were not called into action.

On February 14th 1981, while attending a Saint Valentine Night discothèque, forty-eight young people died and up to 200 received severe burns in a fire at the Stardust Ballroom, Artane, Dublin. There was no formal request for Civil Defence personnel but in compliance with the Major Emergency Plan, volunteers reported to their centres.

In 1982 a Carlow-born poet, Conleth Ellis, published *After Doomsday* in the Raven Long Poem Series. Inspired by a National Fallout Exercise, it began:

> Remember,
> the radio voice intoned,
> you will not see it.
> You will not feel it.
> We have instruments that tell
> us where it is.

After twenty-three pages of imagery as to what could happen, the poem ended:

At the Civil Defence School in 1982. L. to R. Micheál Ó Gabhláin (Chief Technical Officer), Gerry Scully (Director of Civil Defence), The Minister of State at the Department Of Defence, Bertie Aherne T.D. (performing one of his first Ministerial functions) and Eamonn Farrell (School Principal)

To watch the sun wheel behind
its orange cloud
a last time low over the unearthly
red field's
cloak of poisoned grass. The plan
is to wait.

A note explained that two sections of the poem were 'in the official language of the Irish Department of Defence. I have made as few changes as possible in the phraseology of that Department's Civil Defence booklet, *Survival in a Nuclear War*'.

Cosaint Shibhialta donned its favourite blue front jacket for Volume 9 Number 9, December 1982. It gave no indication that it would not appear in its popular form any more. Yet the back jacket quoted from Edward Fitzgerald's celebrated translation, *The Rubáiyát of Omar Khayyám*:

The moving finger writes; and, having writ,
Moves on: nor all thy piety nor wit
Shall lure it back to cancel half a line,
Nor all thy tears wash out a word of it.

SCHISM?

Allegedly, Brendan Behan once commented that the first thing on the agenda of any successful Irish association is a split. The quote came to mind in 1984 when a County Kildare Civil Defence volunteer resigned and set up 'The Voluntary Emergency Service Corps'. Early in 1985, Kildare County Council issued a public statement making it clear that the new organization was not

ZG 5922 (Wicklow AFS)
– one of the former UK
Vehicles purchased in 1989

founded at the request of, or with the consent of the County Council or the Minister for Defence.

GOING TABLOID – THE 'DAILY SPHERE'

An occasional *Network Newsletter* appeared to help fill the gap left by the departure of *Cosaint Shibhialta*, but there was an imaginative issue of the 'Daily Sphere' on Monday August 5th 1985.

'IT's WAR,' screamed a banner headline over a front-page feature that told of a Warsaw Pact invasion of Europe. It was along a 1,000 mile front. Bremen had fallen to Fifth Columnists and Soviet Parachutists but Allied forces had recovered quickly. Maps and photographs accompanied reports.

It was all part of another Civil Defence Exercise.

The National Exercise for the year 1986 simulated a reactor accident and involved the Nuclear Energy Board and the Department of Energy. Coincidentally, the infamous accident at Chernobyl also occurred that year. (See Chapters 2 and 4)

CIVIL DEFENCE NEWS

After six years without a regular house magazine, the first issue of *Civil Defence News* appeared in October 1988. It announced a sensible amalgamation. The Civil Defence Branch at the Department of Defence had moved to Ratra House, bringing administrative, technical and instructional staff under the one roof. At this stage, personnel were speaking regularly on local radio. Travel abroad was becoming commonplace too. Chief Technical Officer Eamonn Farrell and Principal Officer Martin Drew represented the School at 'Exercise Europe '89' held in the French Pyrenees.

Into the 1990s then and members of Dublin Civil Defence visited Wylfa 'A' Nuclear Power Station in Anglesea, Wales, while Kilkenny members attended a Search and Rescue course on the Isle of Man.

On the Fortieth Anniversary of the Civil Defence School, the Minister for Defence, Vincent Brady T.D., planted the first of forty trees in the School grounds. Director of Civil Defence Charles O'Reilly followed suit. Eamonn O'Leary of Dun Laoghaire AFS represented the volunteers in a third planting. He had received 'Rehab. Man of the Year Award' for saving five men and a boy from drowning in Killiney Bay. Other dignitaries did some further digging. That year too, the School conducted its 1,000th course. There was a nostalgic touch, when the retired Micheál Ó Gabhláin, who had been School Principal for so many of those years, delivered an address in the lecture hall. 'It was as if he had never left,' one commentator said.

At the National Auxiliary Fire Service and Casualty Competitions in Bundoran on April 20th 1991, the Minister of State at the Department of Defence, Vincent Brady T.D. issued an appeal for a Civil Defence contribution to the assistance of Kurdish refugees. Within two weeks the organisation had compiled a database of 200 Volunteers. The Irish Red Cross Society, through the International Red Cross, notified the Armenian authorities. However, Tom McKenna of the Civil Defence School Staff accompanied the sixth Irish Red Cross Society relief aid flight to Teheran. He studied the conditions on the ground and recommended sending material aid rather than personnel.

MORE REFUGEES AND MORE EQUIPMENT

In November 1992, most of the national newspapers gave major coverage to the Bosnian refugee situation (See Chapter 2). Their photographers had a 'field day' when Packie Bonnar, the revered

Mr Micheál Ó Gabhláin makes a point in the Civil Defence School lecture hall

Civil Defence volunteers training at the Naval Base, Haulbowline, Co. Cork

Irish goalkeeper, attended a soccer match between a Bosnian eleven and a Renault 19 team on a Tallaght pitch.

Nineteen against eleven? That was a bit unfair!

Kilkenny volunteers received lavish praise for exercising crowd control at the Carroll's Irish Open Golf Championship at Mount Juliet, Kilkenny, in July 1993. Some of the stars, however, had to ask them to keep out of sight when they were putting. The lime/yellow luminous dress was disturbing their eye-line, they claimed. Perhaps it was the handsome features of the Kilkenny volunteers that put them off their chips.

Civil Defence uniforms had been a bone of contention for a number of years. Their blouses worn on ceremonial occasions often displayed an unsightly abundance of shirt at the rear. Eventually, the service received a smart uniform of which it could be proud.

The Service cut a dash in February 1994, when it took delivery of fifteen new high-speed recovery boats and demonstrated skills at sea off the Naval Base at Haulbowline, Cobh.

President Bill Clinton came from the US to visit in December 1995 and up to 200 volunteers from Dublin Civil Defence were engaged in crowd control at various locations.

Boat training off Haulbowline, Co. Cork

In 1997, Wicklow Civil Defence received Brownie points for evacuating and feeding 2000 distressed scouts. Rain had turned their International Jamboree camp near Lough Dan in the Wicklow Mountains into a quagmire.

A group of volunteers from Trim, County Meath visited their twin town, Étrépagny in Upper Normandy and took time to view the World War Two Allied landing beaches.

Those Royal County people never miss a chance of learning more about battle skills. Too many matches against 'The Dubs'!

In 1997 too, the Civil Defence Branch of the Department of Defence struck a medal for presentation to volunteers with long service. On May 1st, at a ceremony in Ratra House, representative groups of four from each county received theirs from the Minister of State at the Department of Defence, Jim Higgins T.D.

Presentation of medals to volunteers with ten and twenty years service by the Minister of State Mr J. Higgins T.D. on May 1st, 1997

Civil Defence members sailing to Scotland and Isle of Man aboard the *Asgard II*

Each county arranged local ceremonies to distribute the remainder.

'Operation Shamrock' served as a reminder of when the concept of emergency aid from a civilian force began. Civil Defence transport assisted a nostalgic journey for former German refugee children who had been accommodated in Ireland after World War Two. The German President attended ceremonies in Dublin. The visitors then boarded fifteen Civil Defence vehicles for transportation to Glencree, County Wicklow, where they had been domiciled from the middle to the late 1940s.

The year 1998 began on a tragic note. On Janury 18th, a twenty-four year old Rescue Service instructor of South Tipperary Civil Defence, Patrick Kennedy from Clonmel, lost his life during a kayak training exercise on the River Suir.

Later in the year, on November 30th, Seamus Brennan T.D., Minister of State, unveiled a plaque at the Civil Defence Centre, Heywood Park, Clonmel. He said that Patrick 'typified the true spirit of Civil Defence'. The Chairman of South Tipperary County Council, Councillor Brendan Griffin described Patrick as 'a true patriot who had willingly and selflessly laid down his life for another'.

Ar dheas Dé go raibh a anam

Up to 1,300 volunteers were involved during *Le Tour de France en Irlande*, 1988

Le Tour de France en Irlande began on July 11th 1998 with a Prologue Time Trial route starting from College Green, Dublin and racing through city streets before ending in O'Connell Street. On the following day, Stage 1 began and ended in Dublin, having taken in a number of scenic diversions in County Wicklow. For Stage 2, the race transferred to an Enniscorthy, County Wexford starting point. Heading for Waterford and up to Sean Kelly's home town of Carrick-on-Suir, it then reversed and ended on the Carrigrohane Straight in Cork.

It was a costly and time-consuming effort for Civil Defence and involved considerable pre-planning. Up to 1,300 volunteers worked from six to ten hours each day.

Two Civil Defence teams competed in an 'international' competition at Bracknell, Berkshire in 1997. Participating in a similar competition in September 1998, a North Tipperary team won, in the Isle of Man (through their experience in de-tailing Kilkenny Cats?) They brought back a silver cup valued at £5,000.

EUROPE, 2000 AND ONWARDS

The Department of Defence conducted Exercise Europe '99 from April 23rd to 26th. Co-ordinated from Dublin, imaginative exercise instructions envisaged an underground explosion at Tara Mines near Navan, County Meath, a mid-air collision between a passenger jet and a light aircraft over Tullamore, County Offaly and a train-car collision at a level crossing near Mallow, County Cork.

A visiting European delegation included observers from Austria, Denmark, Germany, Spain, Finland, France, Greece, Italy, Netherlands, Portugal, Sweden, England, Northern Ireland, Scotland, Belgium, Iceland and Norway. They later outlined their impressions of positive and negative aspects of what they had seen.

The September 1999 edition of the glossy magazine *Galway Now* carried a colourful illustrated feature. Eileen Bennett wrote: 'They're everywhere, those men and women in their fluorescent yellow boiler suits or distinctive black uniforms. Just about every major event, from horse shows to arts festivals, relies on the presence of Civil Defence to ensure that it all happens surely and safely.'

The year 2000 arrived surely and safely too, but amid considerable ballyhoo. RTE screened the last sunset of 1999 at Dursey Island. It was spectacular; almost a spiritual experience. Later on, Joe Dolan sang in the new year. Joe and RTE had many critics. Civil Defence personnel assisted in crowd control at a number of events throughout the country. They received nothing but praise and the odd sore head resulting from PDC (Post-duty Celebrations!).

The wheel had come the full circle when, in March 2000, American Colonel Thomas Ferebee died, aged eighty-one. He was the man who released the first atomic bomb from the US B-29 bomber, *Enola Gay*, to destroy Hiroshima. One obituary claimed that Ferebee never felt any guilt at his action and once said 'Sure, Hiroshima is horrible; but war is horrible... None of us who were on the *Enola Gay* ever lost a minute's sleep over it.'

He went on to explain that without Hiroshima, a land invasion of Japan would have been necessary and quoted estimates suggesting that a million Americans and as many Japanese would have died as a result.

The end of the year 2000 will come a few weeks after the Golden Jubilee of Civil Defence. Perhaps Joe Dolan should be called back to the celebrations. One of his most popular songs was

'Tar and Cement'. It is about big cities and enormous built-up areas. In God or man-made disasters, tumbling cement and falling steel are treacherous. Tar and cement, water and fire, crashes and disasters all cause havoc. Rescue, care and attention in their aftermath need the skills of all Civil Defence services.

If detractors persist, perhaps volunteers should quote the American political activist Eldridge Cleaver (1935-98):

'What we're saying today is that you're either part of the solution or you're part of the problem.'

4

The Army Connection

During World War Two (1939-45) the Army expanded far beyond its peacetime level. Its objective was to repel invaders. There were two major Divisions. The 1st Division would protect the south coast against possible German invasion while the 2nd Division would oppose a British advance across the Northern Ireland border. A subsidiary Army task, provided it was not engaged in its primary responsibility, was to assist the civilian population in bombed areas. A Local Security Force (LSF) existed in designated local areas of An Garda Síochána. Some of its squads specialized in traffic control, communications, protective duties, first aid, transport and air raid precautions. The Air Raid Precautions Act, 1939 instructed Local Authorities to prepare precautionary schemes, but its Section 60 tasked the Minister for Defence with providing services, training and ARP equipment. ARP personnel were forerunners of Civil Defence volunteers.

RAPID TECHNOLOGY

There was always considerable co-operation between Civil Defence and the Army. Some of the instruction imparted to military personnel at the Civil Defence School was later incorporated into training for regulars and reservists. A number of army personnel resigned and took up appointments as CDOs and Assistant CDOs with Local Authorities. Others assisted at drill training and in cooking duties at large summer camps.

Neither Dangerous Dust nor Angel Dust had been heard of in rural Ireland when a young Army training officer with An Fórsa Cosanta Áitiúil was having trouble keeping members of a small rural centre interested in military training. After returning from a short Civil Defence Course at Ratra House, the officer initiated a series of lectures on the subject. The attendance improved. There was a record full house, however, on the night he had announced a particular subject: 'Protection of Livestock in a Fallout Situation'.

There was never any question of the Defence Forces taking on a Civil Defence role in an emergency. In August 1960, An tAire Cosanta, an tUasal Caoimhghín Ó Beoláin T.D. made this clear. He was speaking in Dáil Éireann on the Estimate for Civil Defence for the year 1960-61 and said:

> It has been stated that the Army should do [these tasks]. Such an attitude reveals a complete lack of appreciation of the nature of Civil Defence, which is essentially the organisation and training of the individual citizens so that they may protect themselves, their families and their neighbours from the hazards of nuclear warfare. If such a war comes, the emphasis will be on survival, and unless the people take the necessary steps to protect themselves, particularly in relation to radioactive fallout, survival will not be possible. The Army could not possibly carry out all the functions visualised by Civil Defence.
>
> Many of these functions are similar or analogous to services normally provided by the Local Authorities even in peace time, such as hospitalizing the sick and injured, fire-fighting, re-housing those in need, assisting the destitute – all life and property saving functions performed as part of the normal day-to-day work of the Local Authorities, which in the event of war would need to be greatly expanded. The Army obviously could not carry out these duties. In any event, the primary function of the Army is active military defence and it is organised and trained towards that end. In the event of war, it would have to be greatly expanded to fulfil its primary role and could not undertake direct responsibility for Civil Defence.

OBSERVER CORPS

When the nuclear spectre threw its shadow over the globe, the Army drew up an elaborate structure for a proposed Observer Corps and submitted it to the Government. That was in 1959. There were many amendments before the final establishment of the Corps in August 1961.

The concept envisaged a small cadre of sixty-three Permanent Defence Force (PDF) personnel commanding, controlling and administering a reserve force of 3,772, all ranks. In crews of five, these would man 437 Observer Posts, situated fifteen to twenty miles apart. They would also man eight Group Centres and three Sector Controls countrywide as well as a National Control Centre. Volunteers would form a separate Reserve Force from An Fórsa Cosanta Áitiúil.

For a while, Portlaoise was under consideration as a location for Corps headquarters. In 1966, however, work began on preparing the basement of Army Headquarters in Infirmary Road, Dublin for the purpose. Its use as a temporary National Control Centre was also under consideration.

The Army Corps of Engineers extended the basement and installed a roof of massive, fourteen inch thick concrete slab. Then they continued with blockwork and plastering. The work was completed in 1969. The building later served as a control centre for refugees.

ELECTRO-MAGNETIC PULSE

In 1984, there was increasing awareness that the country's communication facilities and equipment were not protected against the burst of radio energy that would follow an explosion. This was known as electro-magnetic pulse, or EMP. The Government set up an inter-departmental committee to study the problem.

A three-phase plan emerged that aimed at activating the Observer Corps, equipping it adequately and training 800 FCA personnel within two years.

It made economic sense to replace existing equipment rather than take on the expense of protecting it against EMP.

RESTATING ROLE

In 1987, representatives from the Observer Corps, Civil Defence and the Department of Defence formed a board to assess National Warning and Monitoring Requirements. Its findings restated the Observer Corps role as follows:

> The Observer Corps will, through a network of observation posts throughout the country, detect explosions, if any, on the State or it's environs and the first arrival of fallout, communicate their findings rapidly through intermediate levels to National Control, process these findings to give a fast national picture, in broad brush strokes, of Gamma Radiation effecting the country and lay the basis for subsequent warnings by civil and military authorities.

SOME PROGRESS

By 1988, the Observer Corps had issued GZIs, BPIs and FSMs to 100 monitoring locations in the country. Officers had attended courses conducted by the United Kingdom Warning and Monitoring Organization (UKWMO). Jointly with Civil Defence, Corps instructors conducted courses at its own headquarters and at unit level. These produced trained Warning Officers, Post Crews and Post Crew Instructors. The Corps, using its trained FCA personnel, carried out nuclear fallout exercises in conjunction with simultaneous United Kingdom and French manoeuvres.

However, remote control equipment that could transmit data automatically from unmanned sites was emerging in other countries and would replace unwieldy schemes that demanded considerable manpower.

AMALGAMATION

The year 1998 brought an amalgamation of the Directorate of the Observer Corps with the Directorate of Reserve Forces at Coláiste Caoimhín in Glasnevin, Dublin. In conjunction with the Radiological Protection Institute of Ireland (RPII), it maintained a Radiological Monitoring Section for checking on environmental background radiation. This Section had a number of functions such as detection of nuclear bursts, path prediction, provision of a limited emergency meteorological service and warning neighbouring countries of any nuclear burst detected.

The Section's definitive tasks were formalized in the National Emergency Plan for Nuclear Accidents.

REGIONAL CIVIL DEFENCE OFFICERS

In 1961, after studying a regional organization for Civil Defence, the Department of Defence decided that Central Government could facilitate communication with each Local Authority in wartime by designating a

Regional Controller of defined areas. This led to the secondment of eight senior officers from the Army to act as Regional Civil Defence Officers (RCDOs). They were appointed on June 12th 1961 and took up duties in the autumn of that year. In a note for An t-Aire Cosanta, the Secretary of the Department of Defence stated: 'These army officers have specific responsibility for planning and study of regional control. One of their primary functions is to give the fullest possible advice and assistance in Civil Defence matters to the Local Authorities within their regions. They will work in co-operation with County Managers and other officers of the local authority'.

The eight Regional officers operated mainly in the areas of recruitment, training and organization in a non-executive capacity.

At a conference in the Civil Defence School during September 1961, Local Authority Managers met their new RCDOs. During the early years, there were some slight changes but from February 1st 1973 counties and areas within regions were as follows:

> Number One. Cork North, Cork South, Cork West, Cork City, Kerry.
> Number Two: Clare, Limerick, Tipperary North.
> Number Three: Galway, Mayo, Roscommon.
> Number Four: Donegal, Sligo, Leitrim.
> Number Five: Longford, Offaly, Westmeath, Laois.
> Number Six: Cavan, Monaghan, Louth.
> Number Seven: Kildare, Meath, Dublin, Wicklow.
> Number Eight: Carlow, Wexford, Kilkenny, Waterford City, Waterford County, Tipperary South.

During the crisis involving refugees from Northern Ireland The Department of Defence appointed an additional Army commandant to act as Liaison Officer linking the Regional Civil Defence Officers with Civil Defence Branch. His attachment to the Civil Defence School continued until the practice of appointing Regional Civil Defence Officers ceased in 1992.

Commandant General Sean MacEoin inspecting troops in Athlone Barracks after taking over from the British in 1922

CUSTUME BARRACKS

Like the Civil Defence School at Ratra House, the National Control Centre is located in another historic building. After a storm destroyed Athlone Castle in 1697 a building erected on the site of today's army barracks formed what was known as The Infantry Barracks. By 1837, when a new Queen of England had ascended the throne, it was a comprehensive establishment. It took her name and became Victoria Barracks. More extensions were added in the course of time.

Following the War of Independence and the emergence of a new State, Commandant General Sean MacEoin, the celebrated 'Blacksmith of Ballinalee' took over the building from the departing British troops under Colonel Hore, on February 28th 1922. He re-named it Custume Barracks after the gallant Sergeant who had stormed the bridge across the Shannon in 1691.

Among improvements added by the Army Corps of Engineers over the years was a large four-storey accommodation block. Completed in 1956, its foundations were on an ancient esker and a basement constructed on them eventually became the Civil Defence National Control Centre. That was in 1969.

5

Firmount House

One County Kildare Civil Defence installation has a history worth mentioning. An Anglo-Norman family from Turbotstown House, County Westmeath had many of its line in religion. Thomas Dease (1558-1652) was a professor at Sorbonne, Paris before becoming Bishop of Meath (1621-52). Later in that century, his nephew, Oliver, was Vicar General of the diocese. Saint Oliver Plunkett (1625-1681) was also a relative. A later Oliver Dease was a surgeon who resided at Stafford Street, now Wolfe Tone Street, Dublin and served in the British Navy, probably under a false name. His brother, Richard, lived at Firmount House, Clane, County Kildare from 1794 until his death in 1838. Oliver and his wife Anne were in Firmount House when their daughter, Ellen, was born. Ellen grew up and received education in France and Italy. Her biographer, Kathleen McGovern tells how she was an accomplished musician who was fluent in languages and 'a very well educated, cultural lady, according to the Victorian ideals.'

Returning to Dublin, Ellen joined the Institute of the Blessed Virgin Mary, better known as the Loretto nuns, in Rathfarnham. They later dropped one 't' in Dublin but retained it in Canada. Ellen Dease travelled to that country immediately after her profession in 1847. She was then Sister Mary Teresa. With the assistance of four other nuns, she founded the Loretto order in Toronto and went on to establish thirteen more branches in North America.

Throughout the nineteenth century, tuberculosis became a major cause of death in Ireland. Epidemics continued into the twentieth century and it became known as the 'Irish Disease'. In 1908, the Tuberculosis Prevention (Ireland) Act established hospitals for the treatment of the malady. It also authorized County Councils and Borough Corporations to provide clinics and sanatoria. One of these was at Firmount House.

During World War One, repatriated British soldiers who had been wounded, were returning from the Western Front in such numbers that the Curragh Military Hospital authorities had to

Firmount House

seek extra accommodation. In June 1917, they placed forty beds in Firmount and attended to almost 400 patients there within a year. It became popular. After a spell in Firmount, patients were reluctant to move elsewhere for treatment. Colonel O'Sullivan of the Royal Army Medical Corps reported to his superiors, '[They] always returned ... full of praise and gratitude for the kindness and good treatment they received. It has been difficult to get [them] to again accommodate themselves to the conditions of the ordinary military hospitals such as the Curragh.'

Doctor Noel Browne T.D., Minister for Health in the first Inter-Party Government (1948-51) launched a major campaign to eradicate tuberculosis and Firmount reverted to its former function. Taking the name of Kildare's patron saint, it became Saint Conleth's Sanatorium and continued as such until 1961.

The following year, Civil Defence and Dublin Corporation

inspected the building. They were considering it as a County Control for Dublin or as a Regional or National Control. On November 15th 1963, the Secretary of the Department of Defence wrote to the Secretary of the Office of Public Works (OPW, former Office of the Commissioner of Public Works) announcing the Department's intention to rent Firmount House from Kildare County Council. M.D. Doyle, the OPW architecht inspected the house and reported the presence of *merilius lacrymans*, better known as dry rot. The roof was leaking and the basement had suffered a severe attack of woodworm. Undaunted by the report, the Department considered that the condition would not rule out the premises if a 'method of maintenance was devised to keep the fabric of the building free from dampness and well ventilated'.

A later inspection revealed that Kildare County Council had carried out a 'good job of eradication of dry rot'. Its spread could be further arrested by spending a sum of £750.00 The basement was again considered as a National Control Centre but its condition and an estimate of the cost of putting it right finally eliminated it from further consideration.

In 1964 the Department of Defence purchased Firmount House from Kildare County Council for a sum of £10,000. In 1966, it became Dublin County Control, Kildare County Control and also Number Seven Regional Control.

6

Competitions and Exercises

During the 1970s and the 1980s, County, Regional and National Competitions provided popular stimuli to Civil Defence training. Leaders and volunteers were highly motivated to excel and bring honour to the town or village they represented. Only success in Gaelic games was more important, it often seemed. Sometimes rivalry and tensions were so intense that allegations of cheating arose. An enthusiastic amateur film-maker had his camera on a tripod shooting the action at a Rescue Service competition. The testing panel had hidden their 'casualties' expertly in debris to make discovery difficult. When his home team discovered their 'victims' quickly, the unfortunate cameraman stood accused of pointing his lens towards the place where 'casualties' lay.

Regions hosted the events. The Regional Civil Defence Officer was over-all controller. He sought and booked competition sites and accommodation for the large numbers of officials and competitors. The week-end event normally concluded with a dinner, the awards ceremony and dancing.

NATIONAL EXERCISES

When, in 1992, inclusive exercises were established on a regular basis, the Department of Defence decided on themes and set down broad training parameters for the three Civil Defence Exercises that constituted the National Programme for each year. It selected themes embracing learning points and regimes that would help develop the organisation along planned lines. The Department then appointed two, three or four Local Authorities to host the activities.

Each host Local Authority, working with the Department's representatives, designed and conducted a programme of exercises to meet the needs of the organization. Ten other Local Authority teams up to twenty strong visited each location and participated in devising the programme.

The host Civil Defence Officer relied to a great extent on his

County Kildare AFS in action at Monasterevin, 1966

or her project team. The team normally consisted of ten to twenty volunteer officers who could offer expertise and experience. As work progressed, this group expanded, co-opting experts from outside Civil Defence to handle particular facets of the emerging programme. The hosts maintained the momentum until the completion of the task.

Conducting such an exercise normally required about 150 volunteers. Their commitment in time, energy and ideas was considerable and was a vital requirement.

By the year 1999 most of the country's Local Authorities had hosted a National Exercise. They derived enormous benefits from the experience, learning practical skills and organizational techniques. The establishment of good working relationships with primary responding services at planning level was invaluable.

Each participant was expected to have core skills. The theme or themes of an exercise dictated requirements for additional specialist adeptness. A number of workshops helped in introducing new expertise and techniques to the organization. Civil Defence sometimes conducted the workshops but more often, associated external bodies obliged. These included An Garda Síochána, Regional Health Boards and other primary emergency services.

Provided safety considerations did not dictate otherwise, exercises were open to the general public. Civil Defence policy recognised the desirability of displaying its own expertise. Guest

Combined services exercise at Heuston Station sidings 1987

observers or specialist participants included representatives of Local Government, and other emergency organizations from home and abroad.

The Civil Defence Services always encouraged cooperation with colleagues in Northern Ireland, who received a particularly hearty welcome at exercises.

ON SCREEN

National Fallout Exercises began in 1976. The first to incorporate television broadcasting took place in 1979. Based on the experience gained from it, National 'Network' Exercises have featured in the Civil Defence calendar since 1979. These simulated situations that could evolve if significant nuclear fallout arrived in Ireland. All information available regarding the location, direction and radioactivity level of the fallout was processed at National Control in Athlone. Broadcasts to the nation came from the studio installed there.

The exercises confirmed the need for repeated rehearsals before a national warning and monitoring organisation could perform efficiently.

Initially, radiation reading simulation presented a problem when devising an exercise. Screening meter readings on Radio

An exercise at Heuston
Station sidings 1987

'You're wanted on the phone!'

Telefís Éireann (RTE) during the early hours of a Sunday morning before normal programming hours overcame this.

Exercise participants followed standard drills for logging and reporting readings. The radiological information filtered upward through the levels of control. Meter readings from 350 monitoring stations of An Garda Síochána and from lighthouses around the coast supplemented Wardens' information. The Meteorological Service provided weather information for SOs. RTE became further involved when the exercise included radio broadcast of warnings to the public.

Direct contact with members of the Warden service was an important feature of the 'Network' exercises. They received code numbers by post before the exercises. These related to the wardens' understanding of the data later screened on television.

WELCOME 'COMRAD'!

The 'Comrad' (Communications/Radiation) exercise also became an annual event. It was a National exercise but it concentrated on the upper levels of control and on the international exchange of information.

7

'There's no school like an
old school'

RATRA HOUSE

The celebrated architectural draughtsman, James Malton,
whose Indian ink drawings of Dublin published in 1792 are
still cherished, once criticised the location of the 'Palace of the
Viceroy'. It was in the commercial area of the city around Dame
Street. Much earlier, in the seventeenth century, it had been in
Kilmainham, in a former Priory of the Monks of St John of
Jerusalem. Its exposed position left it vulnerable to attacks from
the O'Tooles and O'Byrnes and it was vacated and leased to Sir
Edmund Fisher in 1611. The Priory had vast tracts of pasturage. At
a place called Fionn Uisce, where the Magazine Fort now stands,
Sir Edmund built a new house. Seven years later, the Government
paid him £2,500 compensation and took it over as the official residence of the King's Representative in Ireland. The Earls of Essex
and of Stafford lived there as well as Oliver Cromwell's son,
Henry. By the early eighteenth century, Fionn Uisce had been
anglicized to 'The Phoenix' and the lands around it became
known as 'The Queen's Garden at the Phoenix.' The Duke of
Ormond made this a deer park and, in 1745, the Duke of
Chesterfield contrived its present layout.

In 1782, work began on converting a former ranger's lodge into
a suitable residence of the Lord Lieutenant or Viceroy. This Vice
Regal Lodge would later become Árus and Úachtarán, the house
of the President of Ireland.

The Viceroy was the senior member of the Irish Executive.
His Chief Secretary lived close by, in the present American
Ambassador's Residence. The former residence of the Papal
Nuncio, since demolished, housed the Under Secretary. The Lord
Lieutenant's Private Secretary lived at the 'Little Lodge', now
Ratra House, the Civil Defence School.

Built c. 1786, the residence was of two storeys. Downstairs
there was a porch and cloakroom, two dining rooms, two drawing
rooms, two breakfast rooms, pantry, kitchen, larder and maids'

The 'Little Lodge'

room. There were nine bedrooms and two bathrooms upstairs. A large conservatory and extensive verandah stretched along an external wall. The roof covered a quarter of an acre.

SCANDAL

Had there been tabloid newspapers in the late nineteenth century, the 'Little Lodge' would have featured in the story of a high society scandal of such magnitude that the Queen saw fit to intervene.

It began when the Prince of Wales took twenty-six year old 'Sporting Joe', husband of Lady Edith Aylesford to India. Pugilism and cockfighting were among this Earl of Aylesford's pursuits. The abandoned Edith was very beautiful and she received prompt attention from the Marquis of Blandford, eldest son of the 7th Duke of Marlborough. Word spread to India that Blandford had left his wife and family to pursue his amorous adventure and Lord Aylesford initiated divorce proceedings. Blandford's younger brother, Lord Randolph Churchill, decided to intervene. He visited the Princess of Wales and requested her to contact her husband and have him prevail on Aylesford to drop plans for divorce. In case the lady should be reluctant, he reminded her that he had the Crown of England in his pocket. He explained that more than Blandford had fallen under Lady Edith's spell and that he could spill the beans, tomato sauce and all. He told the shocked princess that the Prince of Wales himself had been a suitor of Edith's. Randolph further claimed that he had letters to prove it. Before you could say 'smelling salts' the furious Princess was writing to her husband, rounding on him with accusations of infidelity as well as delivering Lord Randolph's message.

The plan did not succeed, however. An incensed Prince threw down both the letter and the gauntlet. Randolph had been his friend and had behaved in a dastardly manner. A duel might be the only acceptable outcome. In the event, the Prince settled for a complete renunciation of his former friendship with Churchill.

Word of the affair and the ensuing brouhaha reached Queen Victoria. Greatly distressed, she wrote to her Prime Minister, who was Benjamin Disraeli, First Earl of Beaconsfield. Buttering him up with plaudits on his wisdom and tact, she declared 'Her Majesty is confident you will manage this perfectly.'

He did. Without delay or even further ado, he appointed the Duke of Marlborough as Viceroy to Ireland and told him to bring Lord Randolph, his son, with him as Private Secretary. On December 12th 1876, they crossed from Holyhead with their families and households on the mail steamer *Connaught*. *The London Gazette* enthused about the welcome they received at Kingstown (Dun Laoghaire) and along the streets of Dublin.

Lord Randolph Churchill's American wife, Jennie and baby Winston came to Dublin with him. Winston was two years of age. The baby's nurse, Mrs Everest, came too. She was to become Winston's friend and confidante until he reached the age of twenty.

FEAR OF FENIANS

The Churchills lived at the 'Little Lodge'. Winston's younger brother John was born there in 1880, just before the family returned to England. There are claims that Winston Churchill often remarked on how his fascination with militarism, particularly cavalry, came from viewing parades in the Phoenix Park. The horse cavalry would have been moving from Marlborough Cavalry Barracks in Blackhorse Avenue (now Mc Kee Barracks) and passing the gate of the 'Little Lodge' on their way to the parade ground near the Phoenix monument. In his autobiography *My Early Life* (London 1930), Winston recalled 'a great black crowd, scarlet soldiers on horseback, strings pulling away a brown

shiny sheet' when his grandfather, the Viceroy, was unveiling the statue of Lord Gough. He remembered the burning of the old Theatre Royal on the day he was to have attended a pantomime there.

He said that Mrs Everest was always 'very nervous about Fenians. I gathered these were wicked people and there was no end to what they would do if they had their way. On one occasion when I was out riding on my donkey, we thought we saw a long dark procession of Fenians approaching. I am sure now it must have been the Rifle Brigade out for a route march. But we were all very much alarmed, particularly the donkey, who expressed his anxiety by kicking. I was thrown off and had concussion of the brain. That was my first introduction to Irish politics!'

It was at the 'Little Lodge' too that young Winston 'was first menaced with education.' Mrs Everest prepared him for his first meeting with a governess but on the day she was to arrive he hid in the 'extensive shrubberies – forests they seemed' that surrounded their home. He remembered the lodge as 'a long, low white building with green shutters and verandahs.' As a child he had thought the lawn around it was 'as big as Trafalgar Square' and that the lodge was about a mile from the Vice Regal Lodge. In 1900, as a grown man he was lecturing in Dublin on the Boer War and visited his childhood home. He was astonished to find 'the lawn was only sixty yards across, the forests were little more than bushes' and was only a minute's ride from the Vice Regal Lodge'.

LODGING CONSTRAINTS!

Elizabeth, wife of William Shannon, the American Ambassador to Ireland from 1977-1981 wrote a diary of events that occurred during her stay in the Phoenix Park (*Up in the Park*. Dublin 1983). An entry for January 12th 1978 reads:

> Commander and Mrs. William King came over from Galway to spend the night with us, and while we chatted at dinner I learned some wonderful stories from them about the history of our house.
>
> Anita Leslie King's grandmother was Leonie Jerome, the sister of Jennie Jerome Churchill, Winston's mother. Leonie met her future husband, John Leslie, in this house, at a party given by Randolph and Jennie Churchill. They were living here while Randolph served as private secretary to his father, the Duke of Marlborough, who was Viceroy at that time.
>
> Winston Churchill was a little boy of five and six when he lived here, riding his donkey cart around the lawns and, no doubt, racing up and down the long back hallway as David does. What wonderful ghosts this house must have.

Anita, a writer and social historian, has vivid recollections of her grandmother's stories of the balls, dinners and flirtations that took place at the residence while the Churchills lived here. We tried to figure out the exact spot in the drawing room where Leonie met her future husband. 'She always said she first saw him hiding behind a pillar,' Anita said.

The four Lodges in the Phoenix Park, some with their own gate lodges, and the relative obscurity of the Private Secretary's, often led to such anecdotal confusion.

James Dempsey was gardener at the 'Little Lodge' and his son, also called James, played games with Winston or rode his donkey around the grounds. 'He was a plump little fellow and good tempered,' a seventy-seven-year-old James 'Junior' told the *Empire News* in a 1951 interview.

Young Winston

'REALLY DELIGHTFUL'

As the Truce in the War of Independence was under negotiation in 1921, a very powerful civil servant lived at the 'Little Lodge'. Mark Sturgis had been a Private Secretary to Prime Minister Asquith before Lloyd George took office in 1916. He came to Dublin with his wife, Rachel, and was a little peeved at having no formal title. In effect, he acted as Joint Assistant Under Secretary with Alfred (Andy) Cope, but nobody wished to risk offending Cope by conferring the appellation. Sturgis was very much involved in negotiations leading to Sean MacEoin's release from prison and from the threat of execution in August 1921. Entries in his diaries (*The Last Days of Dublin Castle*. Dublin 2000) express a love of horses and of Dublin social life.

One reads:

> *Sunday 6 March Private Secretary's Lodge:* It is really delightful here with my good friends. Lucky something is pleasant as it's precious hard to see any sign of dawning Victory in this business.

After the withdrawal of the British administration, three Governors General of the new *Saorstat Éireann*, the Irish Free State, occupied the Vice-Regal Lodge. Some of their retinue occupied the 'Little Lodge' on occasions.

MILITARY OCCUPATION

A veteran of the War of Independence in Clare, Major General Michael Brennan, was Adjutant General when he occupied the Lodge in 1926. He continued to live there when he was Chief of Staff from 1931 to 1940. His wife, May, conducted most of the correspondence with the Commission for Public Works. In November 1937 she wrote that the Lodge had been 'in a state of chaos and we would be indeed pleased to get back to normal home life once again'. The chaos came about because the 'Little Lodge' was the last building in the Phoenix Park to have electricity installed. After considerable correspondence, about such matters as who would supply bulbs, the residence was finally connected up to the Electricity Supply Board mains on December 17th 1937. The Brennans had a bright Christmas!

Some old furniture left in the Lodge since the British administration became the subject of some dispute. Eventually, a settlement emerged and, although on holidays in Kilkee, May Brennan wrote to a Mr Shouldice at the Furniture Section of the Office of Public Works complimenting him on the blue rexine he had selected for the Chesterfield suite in the drawing room.

Because an inspector claimed they were in a dangerous condition, there was a move to knock some outhouses in 1940, but the Brennans needed them. They owned 'two cars, a pony and carriage, a cow and sometimes a calf, besides fowl and other domestic animals'. Considerable garden produce, credited to the husbandry of gardener Joseph McCormack, needed storage space too. Correspondence often appeared somewhat critical of the Brennans having free use of a gardener and paying low rent for the Lodge.

When the Brennans vacated the Lodge in the summer of 1940, the Department of External Affairs made enquiries to the Commissioner of Public Works on behalf of the Spanish Government for its use as a Legation. The Commissioner's secretary replied, 'It is in bad repair. Offer it for a rent of £100 but we will not undertake any preliminary work'. World War Two was in progress then and the request came to nothing.

The Plans and Operations Section and part of the Administrations Section of Army Headquarters moved into the 'Little Lodge'. A Commandant Finn sought all sorts of improvements, including the equipping of an officers' mess and ante room. A staff from Messrs Dockrell began external painting but, perhaps on security grounds, the Army authorities requested cancellation of the work. They also requisitioned security gates and floodlighting. The Army finally vacated the Lodge on August 11th 1944.

Meanwhile, the External Relations Act of 1936 had abolished the position of Governor General and when the 1937 Constitution of Ireland created the office of President of Ireland, Douglas Hyde (Dubhglás de hÍde) was the unanimous choice of all parties. His inauguration took place in June 1938.

On the last day of that year his wife, Lucy Comentina, died. He himself suffered a stroke in 1940 and ended his period of office in a wheelchair, tended by his sister Annette and Nurse Kathleen Fitzsimons.

When the end of Douglas Hyde's period as President was in

Douglas Hyde moved ito the 'Little Lodge' on his retirement as President of reland

sight, the war was not yet over. In February 1945 An Taoiseach, Eamonn De Valera T.D., and the President's Secretary, Michael McDunphy decided that, on his retirement, the ailing ex-President and distinguished scholar should move into the 'Little Lodge'. There was considerable renovation and refurbishment and a frustrated J. Connolly wrote on behalf of the Commisioner for Public Works to Maurice Moynihan, the Secretary to the Government. He complained that over £1,000 was spent 'rehabilitating and furnishing', and added: 'We are in the difficult position of having to take our instructions from McDunphy and we are not in a position to challenge or question any of his directions.'

Connolly did, however, manage to have the retiring President pay £118.10.10 for linoleum, carpet, rubber nosing and Holland blinds and agree an annual rent of £165.0.0 for the Lodge and its four acres from June 26th 1945. The lease was to be renewed annually. The firm of Messrs Dockrell managed to complete the painting then too, at a cost of £318.15.0

The ex-President's sister and nurse joined him. In his writings, Dubhglás de hÍde had used the pseudonym *An Craoibhín Aoibhinn* (The Delightful Little Branch). He had been the moving spirit and first President of the Gaelic League. A native of

Castlerea, County Roscommon, Hyde had done most of his writing and organisation of the Gaelic revival at Ratra Park, near Frenchpark. After occupying the 'Little Lodge', he promptly named it Ratra House. He referred to it affectionately as 'Little Ratra' and to his former home in Roscommon as 'Big Ratra'.

One of his many visitors to Ratra House was his first Presidential Aide de Camp, Captain (later Commandant) Eamonn de Buitléir, father of the popular naturalist and film-maker. Hyde's life during that period was distressful. Bedridden, he suffered the discomfort of itching and skin ailments then associated with that condition. He died there on July 12th 1949. Two days later his tricolour-draped coffin left Ratra House for St Patrick's Cathedral.

Expecting a large crowd, the auctioneers charged with disposing of the late President's effects sought permission to use the front paddock of Ratra House as a car park but were refused. They also received a reminder that the fire extinguisher, garden seats, fixed curtain pelmets and kitchen table belonged to the Commissioner of Public Works and should not be offered for sale.

SELECTION

During the following year the Department of Defence was considering the suitability of various buildings as headquarters for Civil Defence. Montrose House, now occupied by RTE, was among them. Ratra House was the final choice and the organization began establishing its Headquarters and School there. The house had altered little since it was the home of the Private Secretary. The drawing room, dining room and main bedroom were of generous proportions, but others varied in size, some being little more than cubby-holes. Despite the numerous pleas from the Brennan family during their occupation, little had changed structurally.

The study, day nursery, larder, butler's pantry, scullery, drying room, night nursery, sewing room and maids' quarters still recalled days of gracious living. Steps down from the impressive Victorian conservatory led to pleasant gardens.

Because of the preparations for the retired President, however, the building was in good condition. In January 1951, an architect from the Office of Public Works inspected it. He recommended new toilets on ground level, fenders, fire irons, fuel bins and, ashtrays! Noting the proximity to Áras an Úachtarán, he expressed concern at the possibility of loud noises or explosions during outdoor training.

CIVIL DEFENCE HEADQUARTERS STAFF

The Civil Defence organization included both administrative and

technical personnel. It adopted the dual management system used
in other areas of the public sector. Initially, Ratra House did not
accommodate the full complement of staff. An administrative section functioned there, as did the School Commandant (later
called School Principal), and instructors. The Chief Technical
Officer and other technical officers occupied accommodation in
the Red House of Army Headquarters on Infirmary Road.

Ballybruskar

The Official Opening of the School by the Minister for
Defence took place at 9.45 a.m. on Monday June 18th 1951. Oscar
Traynor, T.D. is the first name entered in the Visitors' Book. The
First Course for Civil Defence Officers then began, and lasted
until Friday June 22.

Early courses concentrated on general and rescue training. They
were conducted in the old dining room, later divided to accommodate the Chief Technical Officer and the computer room.

BALLYBRUSKAR

Out offices still standing at Ratra House also reflected bygone
days. They included a potting shed, coach house, stables, straw
store, horse box, meat safe, carriage house, stableman's loft, hay
loft, cow byre, fowl and calf houses. Some of these were incorporated in a training range constructed by the Army Corps of
Engineers during 1952-3 at a cost of £7,950. It included an incendiary bomb hut, a gas chamber, a decontamination range and a gas
compound. The idea of adding a wrecked village with its own
Automobile Association signpost pointing to Ballybruskar (The
town of the Rubble) delighted press reporters. Bold headlines
proclaimed:

Main Street,
Ballybruskar

IRELAND WILL BUILD ITS OWN BOMBED
VILLAGE
CHURCHILL ONCE PLAYED IN 'A-BOMB' GARDEN.
BUILDING A SHAMBLES
STATE TO SPEND £20,000 ON THEIR DESERTED
VILLAGE

The Corps of Engineers also built four garages at the bound-
ary wall with Áras an Uachtarán. They rebuilt a gate pier to Ratra
House, after an enormous amount of correspondence as to who
knocked it!

All Departmental Estimates in the early years of Civil Defence
sought sanction for a further thirteen training ranges throughout
the country. The estimated cost would be £27,000. In 1955, the
demand decreased to six ranges costing £2,000 each. The same
Estimates included a sum of £5,000 towards new syndicate rooms
at the School. The Army Corps of Engineers built these. Early
courses had revealed a need for changing rooms and ablutions.
The existing bathrooms were inadequate. There was a proposal to
convert the kitchen into changing rooms fitted with lockers, but a
bolder stroke obviated such a requirement.

LECTURE HALL

On September 26th 1959, the Secretary of the Department of
Defence wrote to the Secretary at the Department of Finance
about 'improving accommodation and training capacity of An
Scoil Cosanta Sibhialta in accordance with the permanent status

The Lecture Hall

now accorded to Civil Defence'. He said that in 1951 the organization's 'period of occupancy was uncertain and was, in fact, regarded as a temporary measure'. Furthermore, the Secretary stressed, early students were predominantly male. Now women were arriving on courses and 'this fact alone necessitates separate locker rooms, dressing rooms and toilet accommodation'.

The Secretary proposed the construction of a new lecture hall adjoining the northern end of the existing building. He estimated the cost at £10,000, but stressed that he considered the expenditure to be absolutely necessary. Time passed and the cost escalated to £18,000 with a further £4,000 for locker and toilet accommodation. Sanction for £18,000 was received on April 26th 1960 and there were suggestions about the Army Corps of Engineers carrying out the work on lockers and toilets.

Tenders were invited and nine contractors, including J. Sisk and Sons, applied. The lowest tender was accepted. It was from Messrs Keegan & Sons, 35-38 Gardiner's Lane, Dublin and stood

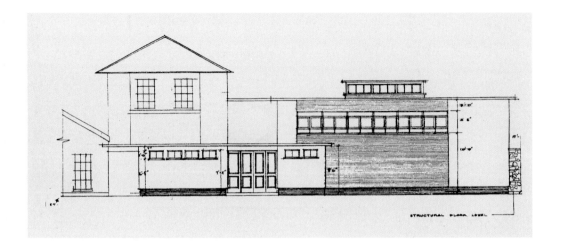

OPW Plan of front
elevation

at £22,150. The firm signed a contract with the OPW on October 31st 1962. In 1963 construction got underway on the lecture hall, adjacent entrance, toilets and a canteen. The architect for the project was F. Duberry with M.F. Crowe assisting and supervising the construction.

The lecture hall was built on the site formerly occupied by the Victorian conservatory. Fittings included a large stage with proscenium curtains and valance, special stage light effects, controlled ceiling lights, blackout curtains and a film and slide projector room. It had considerable flat floor space with raked seating around the walls. This arrangement was useful when floor models were in use, but it isolated the audience from the speaker in a lecture situation. Yet it impressed students from government departments that were still operating with antiquated furnishings and equipment.

Coffee time in the former Private Secretary's drawing room was an enjoyable interlude during courses. A regular Civil Service announcement that each individual's allotment was 'one plain and one curly biscuit' amused early students.

During the 1963-4 construction, locker rooms at the south side of the building and the double door entrance leading to a tiled foyer were completed. A demand arose for a fourth syndicate room and so a wooden floor was laid on the concrete of the existing Rescue Range tower room.

In the 1960s the School came under the control of the technical staff who all transferred to Ratra House.

STORES

The requirement for considerable storage space for Civil Defence equipment necessitated its dispersal over twenty locations. These included internal rooms in Ratra House, two dilapidated build-

Ratra House. A later photograph

ings and two internal stores in Department of Defence Headquarters in Infirmary Road. Plans for proper storage accommodation emerged in 1962. A sympathetic climate for its provision existed, because Civil Defence was then accepted as an essential component of the country's effort to survive in nuclear war. Nevertheless years passed, during which there were protracted but unproductive discussions with the OPW and the Army Corps of Engineers. The use of private consultants was considered at one stage but eventually Civil Defence School staff designed the separate School and Central stores for construction under one contract.

A PLAQUE ON YOUR HOUSE!

M.E. Synon, in the *Sunday Independent* of November 15th 1998 recalled the Winston Churchill connection with Ratra House and decried the fact that it was not marked by a plaque or the like. She wrote 'There should be a room inside with an exhibition about the family's time in Dublin. It would be a suitable thing for the Queen to open when she finally visits: Churchill was, after all, her first Prime Minister.'

Yes, indeed, and perhaps he learned his famous V sign down around the Wellington Monument and tried his first cigar in the potting shed at the 'Little Lodge'!

8

Looking forward

The eighteenth century political writer and orator, Edmund Burke said in his *Letter to a Member of the National Assembly*: 'You can never plan the future by the past.' He was not the only commentator to have regarded history with some scorn. Pondering on the past, however, can help the shaping of a positive attitude to the future. Remembering how things were and how people behaved through good and bad times can be advantageous. Successes can be repeated and built upon while wise counsel can be offered through recalling mistakes.

Civil Defence faces the future with confidence that the first half-century of its existence has established firmly a durable culture of life saving, community service and preparedness for possible disasters. A rapidly changing global society will demand repeated diversification. This will cause few problems to a Service that has developed versatility and imagination in carrying out its duties. The skills and knowledge that current members have acquired are bound with pride in a distinguished past. This leaves them well equipped for adapting to change and for developing a methodology to suit it. They will pass this on to another generation to assist it in whatever challenges it too may face. So it will continue – determination, confidence, courage, loyalty, dedication and true patriotism perpetuating a distinguished and respected ethos.

Nár laga Dia a lámha go deo.

Staff of Civil Defence School 2000

Back row L to R:
W. Horgan, P. Murphy, P. Kennedy, M. Cassidy, T. McKenna, R. Mooney, N.McManus, M. Brady

Middle row:
M. Mooney, F. Haigney, F.O'Hanlon, C.Byrne, M.T. Smith, A. Clarke, E. Gleeson, J. Gallagher, K. Dowling.

Front Row:
P. Creaner, F. Mulcahy, J. Sewell, M.L. O'Donoghue, E.A. Farrell S. Lawless, O. O'Sullivan

Services Structures

Central training of instructors and provision of training equipment for Civil Defence is the responsibility of the Department of Defence. Local Authorities carry out recruiting for and training of the voluntary Civil Defence services. Civil Defence is structured as follows:

WITHIN THE DEPARTMENT OF DEFENCE:

Minister for Defence
Minister of State
Secretary General
Director of Civil Defence
Civil Defence Branch
Civil Defence School

WITHIN THE LOCAL AUTHORITY:

Elected Members
County/City Manager
Civil Defence Officer
Assistant Civil Defence Officer
Civil Defence Volunteer Officers
Civil Defence Volunteer Members

DEPARTMENT OF DEFENCE

The Minister for Defence normally delegates responsibility for Civil Defence to his Minister of State.

The Minister of State at the Department of Defence develops the policy for Civil Defence.

The Secretary General is ultimately responsible for the execution of the policy.

The Director of Civil Defence, acting under the Secretary General, executes the policy.

The Civil Defence Branch is the administrative centre of Civil Defence and provides a source of expertise for the organization.

The Civil Defence School (see Chapter 7) provides training for Local Authority instructors, for officials of Central and Local Government, for personnel from the Permanent Defence Forces and An Garda Síochána. It also provides training for Scientific Officers and conducts other training events and exercises. The School also organizes certain courses and exercises at local centres.

LOCAL GOVERNMENT

Elected Members represents the public on County and Urban Councils and City Corporations.

The County /City Manager has responsibility for Civil Defence within the Local Authority. He normally delegates this responsibility to his Civil Defence Officer.

The Civil Defence Officer plans, organizes and recruits for Civil Defence. He or she facilitates classes, training exercises and competitions but, above all, ensures that the County organization can respond efficiently and effectively when required. Some County Managers appoint their CDO on a full time basis; others settle for a part time officer with the services of a full time Assistant County Civil Defence Officer.

The Assistant County Civil Defence Officer works closely with the CDO and carries out many of the tasks for which the CDO is directly responsible. He or she formulates each Civil Defence Training Class, the basic unit of Civil Defence.

Civil Defence Volunteer Officers hold ranks of Commander, First Officer, Second Officer, Third Officer, Leader and Assistant Leader in one of the voluntary Civil Defence services. Many are Instructors. They wear uniform when on duty.

Civil Defence Volunteer Members come from all walks of life. Some are already members of other Voluntary Aid Societies. They are people with a strong civic spirit and sense of commitment towards serving the community in which they live.

EXPENDITURE

The Department of Defence is responsible for 100% of expenditure required for establishing and maintaining Control Centres at National and Regional levels. It pays 70% of the cost of establishing and maintaining County Controls and other Local Authority expenditure on Civil Defence. The Local Authority pays the remaining 30%.

Headquarters Staff

Commentators in the year 2000 would criticize an early guide to selection of personnel for Headquarters Section as being politically incorrect in the extreme. It advised 'While women will play a big part as section members, the officers will, in the main, be mature men with experience of responsibility and of good education and background'. Originally a uniformed body, Headquarters' structures envisage a wartime situation, when Central Government officials would staff National Control and Regional Control. Each Regional Control Centre would be combined with a convenient County Control. Normally the term Headquarters Staff indicates those manning County Control Centres and would be a combination of selected Local Authority staff and Civil Defence volunteers.

In wartime, the County Manager would become County Controller. His senior officials, including the County Engineer and County Secretary, would play important roles. Volunteers would fill assorted appointments in staffs responsible for Operations and Intelligence, Scientific Intelligence and Communications.

Scientific Officers (SOs) require scientific or technical qualifications in order to advise the County Controller.

County Control Centres need to have a high level of protection against radiation and be capable of housing up to sixty people in wartime. This figure would include the Headquarters Staff, liaison officers from the Defence Forces, An Garda Síochána, Regional Health Boards, Voluntary Aid Societies, Heads of Civil Defence services and of Local Authority departments.

Scientific Officer Eamonn Nash checks fallout movement at Cork South County Control

Auxiliary Fire Service

The Auxiliary Fire Service (AFS) was established to assist regular county or city fire services in wartime. World War Two and other conflicts bore testimony to a high incidence of conflagrations due to air and artillery bombardments. These led to fatalities on a massive scale. Even when lives were saved, destruction of property left thousands homeless. Government planners, therefore, decided on the prudence of having a backup for wartime or other emergencies.

In peacetime, the regular Fire Service deals with most fires and situations seldom warrant pressing the AFS into service. When it becomes necessary – whether for fire fighting, pumping at flood or water supply emergencies – volunteers respond in exemplary fashion and earn the respect of the community involved.

In the formative years of the AFS, the regular Fire Service may have been a little worried that the voluntary service could represent a threat if ever the regulars decided to take strike action. This fear evaporated quickly, however, and in May 1987 Second Officer John Curran could write in *The Firefighter:*

Green Goddesses at the ready

Women firefighters in action

The very mention of AFS was at one time enough to make certain people's hair stand on end! While this phenomenon may still occur on a limited basis, it can be said that attitudes towards the AFS have changed drastically down through the years. This has been achieved to a certain degree through common sense prevailing, but more so because hundreds of AFS men throughout the country have subsequently joined the Retained, Full-time and Airport fire services and many continue to serve in the AFS and pass on the vast knowledge gained to the general betterment of the Service. This has happened to a significant degree in Dublin and indeed many professional fire fighters have encouraged their sons to join. It must be very comforting for parents to know that their sons are in Civil Defence, serving the community and not committing crimes against it like so many of their counterparts these days.

The first fire engines used by the AFS were known as Green Goddesses. Tradition traces the nickname to their resemblance to the green trams of Liverpool, their city of origin. First manufactured in the 1950s, they incorporated features deemed necessary as a result of wartime experiences in England. The 4 x 4 model used by Civil Defence had a 400 gallon tank and a 1,000 gallon per minute pump. Its in-line integral foam inductor was advanced for the period.

Twenty-five new vehicles went into service between 1961 and 1965. Ten more, second-hand, arrived in 1971 when the United Kingdom disbanded its Civil Defence Force. The Green Goddesses gave good service over the years. The AFS received new fire appliances and ambulances during 1981 and the media took due notice.

These Dodge fire engines are up to full fire service standard in every respect. They are painted yellow; a colour recognised as having nuclear and conventional danger connotations.

Each appliance has a main pump, powered by the engine of the vehicle. It also carries a portable, self-operating pumping unit. Its equipment includes ladders, hoses, ropes and all the fittings appropriate to a high standard, modern fire engine. A leader and five volunteers operate it.

WOMEN

Initially, the AFS had separate sections for men and women. Rural areas led Dublin City in early recruitment. The women worked with the portable pump rather than with a full sized fire engine. Nevertheless they were expected to have the same range of skills and techniques as the men.

A factory in a small midland town had a women's AFS unit among its staff. A fire broke out in the factory and the women acted on their own initiative, rushed to the Civil Defence centre and hooked up their portable pump to a small truck that one member had borrowed from her husband. They all sped back to the factory. The driver was of low stature and a startled villager reported seeing a 'scut truck full of young ones tearin' down the street pullin' a dog's kennel. And it had no driver!'

The factory management had followed normal procedure and called out the regular brigade from a nearby town. When it arrived, the fire was extinguished and the women were back at their place of employment. A truck full of young ones indeed! This excellent crew had the last laugh.

Units with a combination of women and men were introduced towards the end of the 1980s.

In AFS training and exercises, simulated fire situations are as realistic as possible. There is tremendous spirit among volunteers and great rivalry at competitions. Anecdotes are sometimes amusing. Because it smacks of falsehood and is a little cruel, one told about the AFS in a southern location must be switched to Galway and surrounds in order to protect the innocent.

Corbett's hardware premises went on fire and the blaze threatened to spread and destroy the centre of the city. The Civil Defence AFS joined the local brigade as other units began arriving from Gort, Ballinasloe and Loughrea. The Civil Defence Warden Service was helping with crowd control. An American visitor strolled down from the Great Southern Hotel on Eyre Square to watch the activity. He was moving in too close and a warden halted him. The visitor said he thought an exception might be made in his case and said so. The warden asked why and

the American replied 'I'm from Boston, Massachusetts. In fact, I am the Boston City Fire Chief.'

XSI 98, Dodge G13 of 1984

The Galway warden looked perplexed for a moment before remarking, 'Well doesn't that beat all! And Tuam isn't here yet.'

John Curran of Clondalkin, Dublin served in the AFS and in the Welfare Service. His unit was in action at a major fire at Dublin's North Wall in 1968. A decade later, there was severe flooding in the Osprey-Willington area of Walkinstown, Dublin. He recalled: 'Three Green Goddesses were mobilized from Dolphin's Barn at around 1800 hours and one that was under repair in Kilmainham was made available at short notice. The task seemed impossible. The water was up to the bumpers on the appliances which, being 4 x 4 vehicles, were quite high off the ground. It was a dark winter's evening and it was raining.'

John told of the progress of the pumping operation, of receiving welcome hot soup, tea and sandwiches from residents and of the joy at seeing footpaths and roads beginning to re-appear as the pumping took effect.

'Any fire-fighter will tell you that one of the worst and least enjoyable task is making up all the equipment after an operation when everyone is tired. It was daylight before the four appliances and their crews made their way back to Dolphin's Barn station, but everyone was in good form and very pleased with a job well done.'

John's account was one of hundreds involving the AFS over half a century. The Service's volunteers give generously of their time in learning skills that can save lives and alleviate misfortune, discomfort or disaster.

Casualty Service

'IF' FOR A FIRST-AID WORKER by William Slator

(From *Cosaint Shibhialta* July 1977)

If you can keep your head while all about you
The roaring traffic thunders past your ear,
If you can swiftly mobilize your helpers
And give the right directions quick and clear;
If you can reassure the suffering victim,
Or by some act of skill, relieve his pain,
If you can improvise a splint and bandage,
That on the broken limb, he'll walk again.
If you can recognize a compound fracture
And pressure points all round identify;
If you can take the patient's pulse correctly
And all the bandage knots securely tie,
If you have got this knowledge and experience
In case of need to do the proper thing.
The chances are you'll never have to use them
But if you do, what happiness you'll bring.

A Casualty Service team in
action

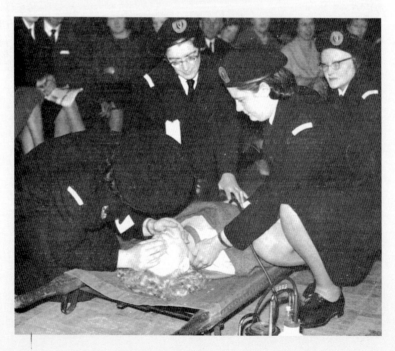

Missing the bus!

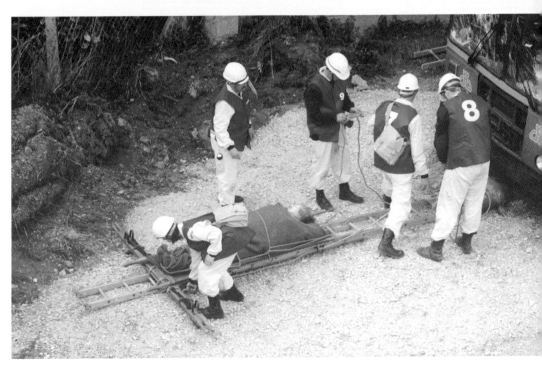

ASSISTING HEALTH AUTHORITIES

The formation of the Casualty Service began on August 8th 1959. It was to be in place in order to assist Health Authorities in the event of war. There was realization that failure to provide prompt assistance to victims of any catastrophe increased the likelihood of serious injury or death.

Members of the Casualty Service are trained to diagnose injuries correctly before applying dressings and bandages. They learn how to give heart massage or mouth to mouth resuscitation. These procedures need no special equipment, but adeptness in applying certain techniques is vital.

Having administered the required treatment, volunteers are required to get their patients to hospital as quickly as possibly in Civil Defence ambulances, which are equipped to a high standard.

Civil Defence casualty training averts tragedies and saves lives at home, in work places, at the seaside and in other situations. Whenever Civil Defence Casualty units and ambulances attend local stock car races, point-to-point meetings, football or hurling matches, they are providing a practical service to the community. At the same time, they are gaining important 'hands on' experience that will advance their efficiency in the event of major disasters.

Civil Defence Casualty units participate in comprehensive exercises to practise co-operation with colleagues in the other Civil Defence services. These exercises often include cooperation with the regular Fire Service, the Ambulance Service, An Garda Síochána, the Order of Malta, the Irish Red Cross Society, St John Ambulance Brigade and others. Some members of these voluntary aid organisations also operate as Civil Defence units.

Part of Henry ('Light Horse Harry') Lee's funeral oration on the death of George Washington might be stolen in tribute to the Civil Defence Casualty Service volunteer: 'A citizen, first in war, first in peace, and first in the hearts of his countrymen.'

*'Very realistic, Volunteer
Bush, but don't over do it!'*

Rescue Service

The Civil Defence Rescue Service provides volunteers trained to release people trapped in damaged buildings or other dangerous situations and to administer basic first aid. Its members learn that loss of life from disaster, whether in times of war or peace, often occurs because expert assistance is not available promptly. Rescue attempts by untrained citizens, however well intentioned, can harm rather than help a victim. The chance presence of a trained Rescue Service volunteer at the scene of an accident could avert tragedy.

Strenuous rescue work demands considerable strength and stamina. Adequate training in the use of rescue apparatus and techniques is vital. The use of ropes and stretchers in conveying the injured from debris, from heights or from basements needs alert minds that will conceive methods of improvisation, when necessary. Although Rescue Service teams have their own transport, they must be prepared to carry their gear in back packs – called man-packs – for long distances over rough ground.

An early Light Rescue team moving into Carlow

While in wartime, rescue teams would be assisting people trapped in their own houses, Civil Defence volunteers are exercised in many other possible situations. These can involve working in quarries, caves, industrial premises or rock faces. Realistic simulated exercises feature aircraft, motor or train crashes, explosion hazards and collapsed buildings.

Rescue teams regularly are in the news for rendering practical assistance to their communities. They rescue people and animals trapped on cliffs and ledges. They often endure the unpleasant tasks of searching for missing persons or recovering dead bodies. Tactful consideration for the distraught or the bereaved is required in such situations.

An anecdote attributed to many sources has also been told regarding a Civil Defence Rescue exercise in the North-East. The Casualty Make Up unit had tagged a supposed victim of a simulated air crash in a wood. The label read 'Bleeding to death'. After a couple of hours, nobody was coming to the volunteer's aid and he was ravenous. Eventually he succumbed to the hunger pangs and deserted. He was thoughtful enough, however, to amend the message on the label before tying it to the branch of a nearby tree. It now read 'Bleeding to Death. Gone home to my dinner.'

Rescue personnel themselves have suffered from hunger pangs on occasions, but they earned a reputation for sticking to their job until it was completed. Solid, dependable people; as the saying goes, 'They won't tear in the plucking.'

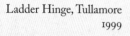

Ladder Hinge, Tullamore
1999

Warden Service

The Civil Defence Warden Service operates in close contact with the public. During national exercises, its members knock on doors distributing literature. Some listen to comments ranging from cynicism to ridicule. The long serving Chief Technical Officer, Micheál Ó Gabhláin summed up the attitude in *Cosaint Shibhialta* of October 1977:

NOTHING EXCEEDS LIKE EXCESS

We often come across an opinion which if it were to be expressed openly (it usually isn't) would run something like this:

'Do you mean to say that after all these years, you people at the School are still talking about nuclear weapons, radioactive fallout and all that outdated stuff?'

It seems that we have gone on crying wolf for far too long. The wolf never came and the conclusion now seems to be that he doesn't exist. Twenty years ago, people were concerned about the threat posed by nuclear weapons although this was accompanied by the fatalistic view that if 'it' did happen there was nothing Civil Defence or anyone else could do about it. Nowadays the opinion seems to be 'it didn't happen; it can't happen; it won't happen'.

DIFFERENT

The Warden Service is the main component of Civil Defence for warning and monitoring at local level in a fallout situation. So its members remain in their own areas and do not operate in teams like the other services. A Warden's beat is a specifically defined piece of territory. He lives in it and knows its topography and its people. Permanent residence is particularly desirable.

Because of this requirement and the nature of the work, wardens are usually older and more settled than members of other Civil Defence Services. They also tend to remain longer in the organisation and there is constant movement from other services into the Warden Service. Many wardens have served for over twenty years , whereas the other services have a rapid turnover in membership.

The functions of the Warden Service falls under three headings:

Warning
Monitoring
Local leadership

The territorial organization of the service is important.
Monitoring, for example, requires taking radiation readings from
points spaced three to four miles apart. That and other factors are
taken into account when establishing units.

An evolved organization meets all requirements for a successful Warden Service. It has the following pyramidal structure:

National Control
Regional Control
County Control
Sub-county
District
Warden post
Patrol

Officials of the Local Authorities or Central Government staff
upper levels, but Warden Service volunteers man Sub-county and
lower levels.

Training covers the taking of radiation readings at Warden
Post and District levels. In rural areas, these correspond respectively to District Electoral Divisions and Dispensary Districts.
The Patrol Warden is the link with the public and he is expected
to embody the function of local leadership for a small area of three
or four localities or for a city street. National exercises cater mainly for practising District and Post Wardens.

A warden monitoring

In April 1972, *Cosaint Shibhialta* published a poem, courtesy of the
Wicklow People. It was written by a Post Warden, Jerome Keogh:

THE INVISIBLE ENEMY.

We fight a cruel and heartless foe that we cannot see or hear,
With rifles no, nor cannons, tanks nor aeroplanes, we fear.
An enemy that isn't there till the 'mushroom' clouds rise dark,
Above the furnace pulverised from home, and street and park.

The foe pollutes the atmosphere, through plumes of air to send
Its Gamma rays 500 miles and more, perhaps, downwind.
We fight it by retreating, unlike the wars of yore,
The barricades are there, behind the closed and bolted door.

The blocked-up windows, tables, pillow cases filled with clay,
Less would have saved the Japanese in their cities on that day.
Zero hour! The instrument, little bigger than a pen,

Shows even small degrees of deadly rays, and then,
With water, food, transistors, torches, candles, matches – dry –
All remain in shelter 'till the enemy passes by.

Saint Francis, save the animals that can't be brought indoors!
No Noah's Ark for creeping things, nor for the lark that soars,
We pray that it may never come; that man may fear to wage
A nuclear war 'gainst fellow man, a blot on history's page;
Or better still that God may not allow this holocaust, this harm
Especially to the children and to many more unborn.

The poem may take on a new relevance and may, perhaps, need a
new stanza in the future. Levels of radioactive gas continue to rise
over the country, according to the Radiological Protection
Institute of Ireland. The rise is from a low base, however and is
due to nuclear processing activities in the United Kingdom and in
France. The gas, known as Krypton 85 is of the noble type. Like
neon or argon, it does not react easily with other chemicals.
Therefore there is no commercial system available to eliminate it
from nuclear plant discharges. Since it began measuring in 1993,
the RPII has reported a considerable rise in concentrations of
Krypton 85. So, man-made radioactivity is on the increase and the
requirement for vigilance continues.

D. Moynihan and R. Ryan
attending the National
Warden Exercise in Co.
Waterford, 1975

Welfare Service

By the third year of World War Two, an Emergency Meals Scheme was in place in Dublin city. It aimed at alleviating hardships resulting from fuel shortages, unemployment or destitution. Although the scheme operated under the auspices of the Catholic Social Service Conference, Dublin Corporation subsidized it. There were twenty-seven centres serving 12,000 hot meals daily. Callers paid a nominal sum of two pennies per meal and took it home to eat. The Service considered it important that meals be eaten in the home environment, if possible.

When the Civil Defence organization emerged, wartime experiences dictated the importance of including a competent Wefare Service that would, if required, have two primary roles:

1. Provision of care for the homeless.
2. Establishment of emergency feeding in situations where people were unable to provide cooked meals for themselves.

Preparing a meal on an improvised cooker

Welfare is the Civil Defence service most frequently called into action and the only one to have been mobilized on a national basis. This occurred in the early 1970's when refugees from Northern Ireland fled south. The Welfare Service's involvement was considerable. It provided personnel for staffing reception centres and for coping with problems presented by large numbers of displaced persons living in temporary accommodation. The Welfare teams were highly praised for their efforts.

In 1992 also, during the Bosnian Refugee situation and in feeding Dublin's homeless people (see Chapters 2 and 3), Welfare volunteers gave outstanding service.

An Taoiseach, Albert Reynolds T.D. and Noel Dempsey T.D., Minister of State at the Department of An Taoiseach and Defence with Comdt Studdart, Dublin CDO and members of Dublin Civil Defence at the Bosnian Refugee centre, Cherry Orchard, 1992

DUTIES

Welfare Service members must be prepared for moving at short notice into an institution and taking over available facilities in order to provide a reasonable degree of comfort and hot meals for large numbers of people. Accessories on issue to the Service include some field cooking equipment and utensils, but sometimes it is necessary to construct temporary cookers from materials available locally. The Service is responsible for providing tem-

A Welfare Feeding Unit vehicle

porary sanitation also.

In the 1960s and 1970s, the two Civil Defence Mobile Feeding Units proved most useful. Each had four vehicles. One was a water carrier. Another transported supplies. The other two were mobile canteens. The combination was capable of producing up to 12,000 emergency meals in twenty-four hours.

TUG-OF-WAR

The spirit of Civil Defence Welfare volunteers combines with their humour in getting results. Lilian Enright, Margaret Hogg and Peggy Joyce remembered the first outing of Castleconnell, County Limerick Welfare unit in their 'bull's wool' uniforms and clip-on ties. They wore high heels that were fashionable but unsuitable for the gymkhana field in Crecora where they arrived to provide catering. Members of another unit from Oola were setting up a mobile kitchen.

'We were astonished to see how much fitted into a small trailer: Soyer boilers, dustbins, kettles, brushes, shovels, hatchets, hammers – everything except matches!'

The women found 'plenty of overhanging trees to avoid, plenty of breeze we could face, but no sound surface'. A sheet of tin from the mobile 'Aladdin's Cave' solved that problem and an obliging smoker came up with the matches. High-heeling it through hedges and fences, they gathered kindling wood. No water carrier arrived so they had to go to the well with buckets and fill the ten-gallon Soyer. They had everything nicely set up when they discovered there was no milk. So high heels spiked again across fields. In one, they manipulated several laps, giving chase to a cow. Eventually, they cornered it. The animal was used to being machine-milked and did not appreciate gentle handling by females who attempted to coax a drop from her udder.

The owner came along and managed to get half a jug-full. He explained that he had milked the cow earlier. Still, it might keep up the good name of Castleconnell and Oola until major supplies arrived!

The consignment of milk did arrive and the units had everything ready at the time requested. But nobody came! Not a single perishing patron! The team became downcast.

'Then bliss! Word came that we were needed. We were needed! Great! Ladies needed to make up a tug-of-war team to replace one that had not turned up. We headed down – in our high heels – only to face a team of heavyweight women trained for the job,

'Oh, yes we can!'

Peggy Joyce, Castleconnell Welfare Group, 1976

County Council and Civil
Defence personnel welcoming
regugees to Cork

in their multi-coloured football jerseys, togs and studded boots.'

They lost. Dirty, broken-heeled and dishevelled they envied the neatness of the two men in the unit. 'We headed home, content in the knowledge that we had a team, each member of which would face anything to get the job done.'

REFUGEES

John Curran of Clondalkin, Dublin served in the AFS and in the Welfare Service. He recalled a night in August 1971, when Welfare units from Drimnagh and Walkinstown went to Ratra House for a briefing before speeding to Gormanston, County Meath.

'We travelled in convoy with two mobile canteens, a water tanker and supply truck. Equipment included twelve Soyer boilers. We were shocked to see the crowds [of Northern refugees] lining the roadway down from the N1 to Gormanston Camp and buses parked on each side of the N1. The crowds were so heavy that we had considerable difficulty making our way through.'

In actual situations, undergoing exercises or catering for distressed civilians or the other services, Welfare is the cheerful face of Civil Defence. In his book, *The People's War* (London 1969) Angus Calder described the shelters during the London Blitz. The Dorchester Hotel had converted its Turkish baths, and there were neat rows of beds. A lovely fluffy eiderdown covered one.

'Its silks billowed and shone in the dim light, in pale pinks and blues. One was curtained off and bore a label "Reserved for Lord Halifax".'

The public shelters had only basic comforts, but a spirited camaraderie made up for what they lacked in luxuries. Calder described them:

'Small coal stoves or electric fires had been introduced. Food was usually available in the larger shelters... In some big shelters, full time "shelter wardens" had been installed, with power to expel undesirables. The social life of the shelters was developed, with official support; gramophones, concerts, play readings, discussions on current affairs, religious services, film shows, libraries, even play centres for children, were provided ... One close observer noted that, as quiet nights became more frequent towards the end of 1940, "The shelter crawl became almost as popular a pastime as the old time pub crawl".'

At least, the Castleconnell Welfare unit had no need to provide 'bouncers'!

The cup of tea in the hand was an Irish gesture of goodwill that featured long before Mrs Doyle began pampering Father Ted. The Welfare Service has provided far more substantial sustenance down the years.

For people in distress or simply cold from standing in an icy wind, their steaming kettles and welcoming smiles earn them a claim to being the 'heart of the roll' – the comforting face of Civil Defence.

Appointments

MINISTERS FOR DEFENCE

Oscar Traynor T.D.	1939-1948	James Tully T.D.	1981-1982
Thomas F. O'Higgins T.D.	1948-1951	Patrick Power T.D.	1982-1982
Gen Sean Mac Eoin T.D.	1951-1951	Patrick Cooney T.D.	1982-1986
Oscar Traynor T.D.	1951-1954	Patrick O'Toole T.D.	1986-1987
Gen Sean Mac Eoin T.D.	1954-1957	Michael J. Noonan T.D.	1987-1989
Kevin Boland T.D.	1957-1961	Brian Lenihan T.D.	1989-1990
Gerald Barry T.D.	1961-1965	Charles J. Haughey T.D.	1990-1991
Michael Hilliard T.D.	1965-1969	Brendan Daly T.D.	1991-1991
James Gibbons T.D.	1969-1970	Vincent Brady T.D.	1991-1992
Jerry Cronin T.D.	1970-1973	John P. Wilson T.D.	1992-1993
Patrick S. Donegan T.D.	1973-1976	David Andrews T.D.	1993-1994
Liam Cosgrave T.D.	1976-1976	Hugh Coveney T.D.	1994-1995
Oliver J. Flanagan T.D.	1976-1977	Sean Barrett T.D.	1995-1997
Robert Molloy T.D.	1977-1979	David Andrews T.D.	1997-1997
Padraig Faulkner T.D.	1979-1980	Michael Smith T.D.	1997-
Sylvester Barrett T.D.	1980-1981		

MINISTERS OF STATE

J. Lalor T.D.	1977-1979
.J. Woods T.D.	1979-1981
S. Moore T.D.	1981-1981
F. O'Brien T.D.	1981-1982
B. Ahern T.D.	1982-1982
S. Barrett T.D.	1982-1986
F. O'Brien T.D.	1986-1987
V. Brady T.D.	1987-1991
N. Ahern T.D.	1991-1992
S. Dempsey T.D.	1992-1994
S. Barrett T.D.	1994-1995
J. Higgins T.D.	1995-1997
S. Brennan T.D.	1997-

DIRECTORS OF CIVIL DEFENCE

W.P. Blunden	1950-1956
J.G. Buckmaster	1956-1969
J. Fay	1969-1971
S. O'Croidheain	1971-1973
M.P. Healy	1973-1977
G. Scully	1977-1987
C. O'Reilly	1988-1993
M. O'Donoghue	1993-

REGIONAL CIVIL DEFENCE OFFICERS

Comdt D. O'Sullivan	1961-1964	Comdt M. O'Brien	1961-1975
Comdt T.C. Maher	1961-1968	Comdt B. M. O'Brien	1961-1971
Comdt J. Phelan	1961-1968	Comdt S. Egan	1961-1968
Comdt L. Corr	1961-1968	Comdt F.J. Hyland	1961-1972
Comdt J.F. Gallagher	1964-1969	Comdt P. MacCarthy	1967-1972
Comdt J.M. Ryan	1968-1976	Comdt M.J. O'Dormell	1968-1975
Comdt J.C. Slye	1971-1975	Comdt M. Power	1968-1968
Comdt C. Browne	1969-1972	Comdt P.J. OConnel	1969-1975
Comdt H. Costelloe	1968-1969	Comdt D.A. Black	1972-1976
Comdt R. O'Shea	1972-1976	Comdt L.G. O'Connor	1975-1979
Comdt A.N.Donnelly	1975-1977	Comdt K. Costelloe	1972-1975
Comdt M.T. Higgins	1975-1976	Comdt J. Young	1975-1980
Comdt R.F. Swan	1975-1977	Comdt P.T. McKevitt	1976-1977
Comdt D. O'Regan	1976-1980	Comdt T.P.K. Barry	1976-1980
Comdt P.J. O'Farrell	1977-1980	Comdt F. Colclough	1977-1981
Comdt P.F.Monaghan	1977-1979	Comdt H.F. Johnston	1977-1981
Comdt J.M.R. Keane	1979-1984	Comdt F. Studdert	1979-1984
Comdt J.F. Whelan	1980-1985	Comdt V. Blythe	1980-1985
Comdt J. Prendergast	1980-1985	Comdt J.J. Cummins	1980-1984
Comdt L. Mullins	1981-1985	Comdt L. Coughlan	1981-1985
Comdt L. Kieley	1984-1988	Comdt J.A. Vize	1984-1988
Comdt M.C. Nolan	1984-1988	Comdt J.J. Curley	1985-1988
Comdt P.J. Keane	1985-1988	Comdt E.J. Breslin	1985-1988
Comdt D.J. O'Regan	1985-1988	Comdt F.M. McNamara	1986-1991
Comdt J.J. Killian	1989-1989	Comdt W.O'Gray	1988-1991
Comdt J.N. Kelly	1988-1991	Comdt P. Cooke	1988-1991
Comdt P.J. Delaney	1988-1990	Comdt P.J. Lynch	1988-1991
Comdt M.P. Dunne	1988-1989	Comdt F. Marshall	1989-1991
Comdt P. Archbold	1989-1991	Comdt M. Canavan	1989-1991

*CIVIL DEFENCE OFFICERS AND ASSISTANT CDO'S

County	CDO	Date	ACDO	Date
Carlow	J. Creed	1951-1983	Capt L.M.Dawson	1970-1972
	J. Lane	1983-1986	Capt M.O'Shea	1972-1974
	S. Grogan	1986-	Capt C.Madigan	1974-1976
			J. Lane	1989-1991
			P. Cahill	1996-
Cavan	A. Madden	1951-1957	P.J. Fay	1974-1985
	J. Gallagher	1957-1958		
	J.J. Connolly	1959-1962		
	J.Gallagher	1962-1964		
	B.J. O'Grady	1964-1968		
	P.J. Fay	1968-1969		
	M. Keaveney	1969-2000		
Clare	T. O'Donoghue	1951-1963	L. Griffin	1977-1995
	J.K. Vaughan	1963-1965		
	L. Power	1965-1970		
	J.J. Higgins	1970-1972		
	N. Carmody	1972-1995		
	L. Griffln	1996-		
Cork City	G. Byrne	1951-1951	T. O'Connor	1992-
	P. Humphries	1951-1978	V. Forde	1998
	C. Garvey	1979-1986		1998-
	P.J. Malone	1987-1987		
	T. McCarthy	1987-1988		
	D. O'Mahony	1989-		
Cork North	J.P. O'Callaghan	1951-1963	J. Maunsel	1982-1987
	T. O'Corcora	1963-1987		
	J.Maunsell	1987-		
Cork South	D.S. Coughlan	1951-1964	G. O'Leary	1974-1985
	J.D. Sheehan	1964-1965		
	W. Lynch	1965-1967		
	T. Wall	1967-1985		
	G. O'Leary	1985-		
CorkWest	C. McCarthy	1951-1961	S. O'Mahony	1974-1975
	J. Lynch	1961-1975		
	S. O'Mahony	1975-		
Donegal	B. Larkin	1951-1952	F. McMorrow	1974-1984
	E. Nulty	1952-1961	J. Patton	1985-1996
	K. O'Donnell	1961-1965		
	R. McCarthy	1965-1967		
	B. Griffin	1967-1980		
	Comdt D. O'Regan	1980-1996		
	J.Patton	1996-		
Dublin	M.J. Burke	1951-1960	Comdt J. Moriarty	1988-
	M.W. O Brien	1960-1972	Comdt J. Carnpbell	1988-
	Comdt T. Treacy	1972-1986	J. Walsh	1992-
	Comdt B. Studdert	1986-		
Galway	B. Sugrue	1951-1984	T. Casserley	1986-1993
	J. Shaughnessy	1984-1993		
	T. Casserley	1993-		
Kerry	A.N. Dillon	1951-1977	T. Healy	1964-1965
	M. Forrest	1979-	F. Kerins	1967-1973
			M. Murphy	1974-1999
			T. Brosnan	2000-
Kildare	J. Creed	1951-1983	Capt L.M. Dawson	1970-1972
	R. O'Shea	1983-1986	Capt M.J. O'Shea	1972-1974
	L. Coughlan	1986-	Capt C. Madigan	1974-1976
Kilkenny	T. P.O'Brien	1951-1962		
	R. Murtagh	1962-1984		
	Noel Bourke	1984-		

Laois	D.P. Ryan	1951-1971		
	J. Fitzgibbon	1971-1975		
	T. Burke	1975-1985		
	M. Cobbe	1986-		
Leitrim	T. Stack	1951-1952	A. McHugh	1982-1983
	M. McDonaghFleming	1952-1953	J.Ganley	1983-1992
	M.J.B.F. Lynch	1956-1963		
	J.F. O'Sullivan	1964-1973		
	J. Guckian	1973-1985		
	J. Martin	1992-1992		
	J. Ganley	1992-		
Limerick City	G.J. Killeen	1951-1953	P. McNamara	1985-1986
	T. Collery	1953-1959		
	M. O'Sullivan	1959-1973		
	J. Fitzsirnons	1973-1973		
	Ms. M. Shanahan	1973-1974		
	J. Fitzsimons	1974-197		
	Ms. M. Shanahan	1975-1986		
	P. McNarnara	1986-		
Limerick Co	E. Cregan	1951-1959	B. O'Brien	1996-
	M. Nunan	1960-1963		
	D. Johnston	1963-1971		
	G. Abraham	1971-1974		
	Ms. P. O'Halloran	1974-		
Longford	R.B. Higgins	1951-1954		
	W.B. O'Farrell	1956-1964		
	M. Colreavy	1964-1994		
	J. Martin	1995-		
Louth	F.B. Boyle	1951-1968		
	H. Lennon	1952-1953		
	Comdt. K.C. McCarthy	1968-1985		
	Comdt. James Lally	1986-1988		
	P. Donnelly	1988-		
Mayo	J. Tierney	1951-1957	T.Duffy	1974-1982
	M. Tuohy	1957-1965		
	P. Kilroy	1965-1982		
	T. Duffy	1982-1998		
	J.F. Cahil	1998-1999		
	J. Maughan	1999-		
Meath	J.E. Duffy	1951-1959	M. Fitzsimons	1994-
	M.M. Gallagher	1959-1961		
	J.J. Connolly	1962-1965		
	D. O'Dwyer	1965-1976		
	LT Col J. Crowley	1976-1987		
	J. O'Grady	1 987-2000		
Monaghan	D.P. O'Conor	1951-1959	P. Reilly	1984 -1996
	J.G. O'Sullivan	1959-1962		
	J.V. Neary	1962-1962		
	S. Finan	1962-1996		
	P.Reilly	1996-2000		
	B. Buckley	2000-		
Offaly	P. Farrelly	1951-1951	J. Gibbons	1965-1970
	D.P.Ryan	1951-1964	N. Coyne	1971-
	J.Hume	1964-1973		
	T. Colville	1973-		
Roscommon	E. Geraghty	1951-1951	S. Maguire	1976-1980
	C.J. O'Connell	1951-1954	D. O'Dwyer	1982-1983
	M. Allen	1957-1969	J. Friel	1983-1983
	V. Brennan	1969-1972	M.J. Cunnane	1985-1990
	W. Kilmartin	1972-1990		
	M.J. Cunnane	1990-1996		
	P. Gallagher	1996-		

Sligo	T. Stack	1951-1952		
	M. McDonaghFleming	1952-1953		
	M. Doyle	1953-		
	M.J.P.F. Lynch	1956-1966		
	P.B. Gannon	1966-1972		
	D. Butler	1972-1973		
	S. McManus	1973-1998		
	S. Kavanagh	1998-		
Tipperary Nth				
	R.Parker	1951-1951		
	T. O'Donovan	1951-1962		
	M. Deegan	1962-1963		
	J.C. Finn	1963-1963		
	P.J. Murphy	1963-1966		
	E.J. Gilmartin	1966-1968		
	T. Donegan	1968-1974		
	M. Corcoran	1974-1989		
	L.Daly	1989-		
Tipperary Sth	J. Fogarty	1951-1962	E. O'Neill	1967-1970
	D. O'Dwye	1962-1964	S. O'Dwyer	1970-1974
	E. Bergin	1964-1990	E. Cooney	1974-1978
	E. Cooney	1990-	M. Walsh	1978-1989
Waterford Co	M. Dowling	1951-1962		
	T. O'Donoghue	1962-1967		
	P.J. Walsh	1967-1984		
	C. Bannon	1984-		
Waterford City	M. Dowling	1951-1974		
	C.Cullen	1974-		
	M. McGuire	1974-1984		
	M.A. Gleeson	1985-		
Westmeath	J.L. Woods	1951-1975	P.J.Sheridan	1974-1983
	J.J. Creamer	1975-1983		
	P.J. Sheridan	1983-1986		
	B. Gillen	1986-		
Wexford	T. O'Connor	1951-1986	T.O'Cormor	1978-1986
	G. Willis	1987-		
Wicklow	H.R.H. Sharpe	1951-1958	B. Downes	1974-1983
	T. O'Mahony	1958-1961		
	J. Brophy	1961-1983		
	B. Downes	1983-		

*DUBLIN ASSISTANT CIVIL DEFENCE OFFICERS

Comdt P. Ryan
Comdt M. O'Farrell
Comdt J. Crowley
Comdt Deveraux
Comdt M.L. Mac Aogain
Comdt F.G. McKevitt
Comdt T.C. Loftus
Comdt G. Hegarty
Comdt. B. Studdert

Comdt T. Keogh
Comdt E.P. O'Neill
Comdt W.P. Murphy
Comdt M.J. Dagg
Comdt V.A. McGrath
Comdt H.T. Anderson
Comdt M.J. Sweeney
Comdt M. Finn

Comdt D. O'Suibhine
Comdt T. Treacy
Comdt J.P. Duggan
Comdt R. Maloney
Comdt P. Feeley
Comdt J. Rigney
Comdt A.J. Donovan
Comdt T. Tracey

*MILITARY LIAISON OFFICERS

Lt Col J. Crowley
Lt Col M. Walsh
Lt Col G. Flanagan

Lt Col D. Dwan
Lt Col D. Fogarty

Lt Col D. Houston
Lt Col D. Deasy

* Compiled from incomplete documentation

Bibliography

MANUSCRIPT SOURCES:

Department of Defence documents and correspondence.
Civil Defence School circulars, documents and correspondence.
Office of Public Works documents, plans and correspondence.
Private Secretary's correspondence held at the National Archives Ireland.
Correspondence from the Office of the Governor General held at National Archives Ireland.
Ordnance Survey Maps held at National Archives Ireland.
Certification and correspondence held at Archives North America, Loretto Abbey, 101 Mason Boulevard, Toronto.
Manuscript of research by the late Lena Boylan, Trustee of Castletown House, County Kildare, Headquarters of the Irish Georgian Society and member of Kildare Archaeological Society.

JOURNALS, MAGAZINES, NEWSPAPERS, PAMPHLETS, VTRS:

Copies of *Civil Defence Bulletin* 1957-1960.
Copies of *Irisleabhar na Cosanta Sibhialta* from 1960-1971.
Copies of *Cosaint Sibhialta* 1971-1982.
Copies of *Civil Defence Newsletter*
Civil Defence brochures, leaflets, booklets and display material.
Annual Registers held at the National Library of Ireland.
Hanley, Lt Col Kevin. *The Story of Custume Barracks Athlone*. Athlone 1974.
McGovern, Kathleen I.B.V.M. *Something More than Ordinary* Toronto, undated.
Department of Energy booklet National Emergency Plan for Nuclear Accidents, 1992.
The Lord Mayor's Handbook 1944 held at the National Library of Ireland.
Towards 2000 (Civil Defence VTR)
The Irish Defence Forces – A Handbook, Dublin 1988.
The Irish Times
Irish Independent
Sunday Independent
Irish Examiner
Evening Herald
Empire News
Sunday Tribune
Provincial newspapers.

BOOKS

A Loreto Sister. *Joyful Mother of Children – Mother Frances Mary Teresa Ball* (Dublin 1961).

A Nun of the Order. *Memories of Loreto* (Dublin 1927).

Bowyer Bell, J. *The Irish Troubles* (Dublin 1982).

Boylan, Henry. *A Dictionary of Irish Biography* (Dublin 1988).

Brynn, Edward. *Crown & Castle* (Dublin 1978).

Burne, Jerome (Ed.). *Chronicle of the World* (London 1989).

Calder, Angus. *The People's War* (London 1969).

Churchill, Randolph. Winston S. *Churchill – Volume 1. Youth 1874-1900* (London 1966).

Churchill, Winston S. *My Early Life* (Fontana Edition, London 1959).

Costello, Con. *A Most Delightful Station* (Cork 1996).

Duggan John P. *A History of the Irish Army* (Dublin 1991).

Dunleavy and Dunleavy. *Douglas Hyde – A Maker of Modern Ireland* (California 1991).

Ellis, Conleth. *After Doomsday* (Dublin 1982).

Goraliski, Robert. *World War II Almanac 1931-1945* (London 1985).

Hickey, D.J. and Doherty, J.E. *A Chronology of Irish History since 1500* (Dublin 1989).

Hickey, D.J. and Doherty, J.E. *A Dictionary of Irish History 1800-1980* (Dublin 1980)

Hopkinson, Michael (Ed). *The Last Days of Dublin Castle* (Dublin 1999).

Hutch, Rev D.D. *Mrs Ball – A Biography* (Dublin 1879).

Hutchinson, Anita Leslie. *Jennie – The life of Lady Randolph Churchill* (London 1969).

Mercer, Derek (Ed.). *Chronicle of the 20th Century* (London 1988).

Mitchell, Arthur and O Snodaigh, Pádraig. *Irish Political Documents 1916-1949* (Dublin 1985)

Montague, John. *The Rough Field* (Mountrath, Belfast, North Carolina 1972).

Moody T.W. & Martin F.X. *The Course of Irish History* (Dublin & Cork 1984).

O'Farrell, Padraic. *The Sean MacEoin Story* (Dublin & Cork 1981).

- *The Blacksmith of Ballinalee* (Mullingar 1993).

- *Who's Who in the Irish War of Independence and Civil War 1916-1923* (Dublin 1997).

- *Shannon Through her Literature* (Dublin & Cork 1983).

O'Mahony, Charles. *The Viceroys of Ireland* (London 1912).

Shannon, Elizabeth. *Up in the Park* (Dublin 1983).